Promoting the Values & Virtues of Classical Education

Latīna Ubīque

Volume II

Thales Press Raleigh, North Carolina

This book is the property of:

Latīna Ubīque: Volume II was published in Raleigh, North Carolina for use in Thales Academy, a network of low-cost, high-quality private schools in North Carolina, South Carolina, Tennessee, and Virginia.

First Edition. Written by Winston Brady, Director of Thales Press.Editing provided by Sarah Forrest, Will Begley, Alison Cartrette, Henry Celmer, Colin Smith, Noah Kelley, Tim Flaherty, Katie Flaherty and Holly Wengenroth-Mealer.

Cover photo is *Achilles and Ajax Playing Dice*, a vase from 530 BC; the photo in the Table of Contents is *A View of Trajan's Forum, Rome* by Charles Lock Eastlake (1821

.).

THALES PRESS Thales Academy DEVELOPING CLASSICAL THINKERS THALES COLLEGE

Table of Contents

TRAJAN'S FORUM

Photo by Gabriella Clare Marino (Unsplash)

Section I
Nouns & Verbs

CHAPTERS

The Latin Noun System

LATIN IS AN INFLECTED LANGUAGE, meaning that the ending of each word changes depending on the use of that word in a sentence. In English, word order determines the meaning of a sentence, so that the placement of a word determines whether it is a subject, direct object, or something else. But Latin is more like a puzzle you have to put together, and it is these endings that determine how that puzzle fits together. If the endings alone cannot tell the reader if a noun is serving as a direct object or a subject, then the **context**—the words surrounding that particular word—should help you understand what ideas the sentence is saying.

In Latin and English, a **noun** is a person, place, thing, or idea. In English, we separate nouns according to the type of noun they are–such as concrete or abstract nouns, collective and individual nouns, and so on. We also speak of nouns as having different types of jobs which, in English, are called **cases**. In Latin, there are six cases in all, but we will focus on two of them for now to illustrate the idea of case. (There is technically a seventh case called the locative case, which is for locations. The locative case is used for cities and islands and is rare enough to merit omitting altogether.)

Those cases are like jobs that a noun may do. The name of the case is also the name of the job that noun does: subject case, objective case, and so on. The **subject** is the main actor in the sentence doing the action of the verb, and the subject case (or the nominative case) is used for nouns that serve as the subject in a sentence. The objective case (or the accusative case) is used for nouns that are the direct object or the object of a preposition. A **direct object** is the noun that receives the action of the verb–that is, whatever action the verb is doing, that action is being done to the direct object.

In English, we do have elements of a case system, particularly with pronouns. Think of the difference between *he* (a subject pronoun) and *him* (an objective pronoun), *who* (subject) and *whom* (objective), *I* (subject) and *me* (objective), and other similar examples. But in most instances, the "job" or the "case" of a noun is determined by word order. That is, wherever the noun is placed in a sentence tells the reader what the job of that noun is. Notice the sentence: *The boy hit the ball*. The subject (*boy*) and the direct object (*ball*) are obvious on a first reading. However, if we switch *boy* and *ball* so that we have the sentence, *The ball hit the boy,* the sentence means something entirely different. In English, word order plays a large part in determining the meaning behind a particular sentence.

BIG IDEA

A noun is a person, place, or thing that, in Latin, is broken down into two parts: the stem and the endings. The stem is what the word actually means (like boy*), whereas the ending tells the reader information like the job that noun is doing in a sentence, how many of the noun in question there are in that sentence, and the gender of that noun.*

Vocabulary

Noun
A noun is a person, place, or thing.

Case
A way of identifying a noun by the kind of function it serves in a sentence. In Latin, there are six cases overall.

Subject
The main actor in the sentence and the person, place, or thing doing the action of the verb.

Direct Object
The noun or pronoun that receives the action of the verb.

Ending
The part of the noun that changes and tells you how that word is used in a sentence.

Stem
The part of the noun that does not change.

Nominative Case
The nominative case is used to signify subject-nouns.

Genitive
The genitive case is used to signify possession.

Dative Case
The dative case is used for indirect objects, the noun that indirectly receives the action of the verb.

Accusative Case
The accusative case is used to signify direct objects, as well as objects of a preposition.

Like verbs, nouns are composed of two parts: a stem and the noun ending. The **stem** is the part of the noun that does not change. The **ending**, meanwhile, does change to indicate how that particular noun is used in a sentence. Let's start with the noun *puella*, meaning "girl." If the word *puella* appears in a sentence, it is being used as a subject, as in the diagram below:

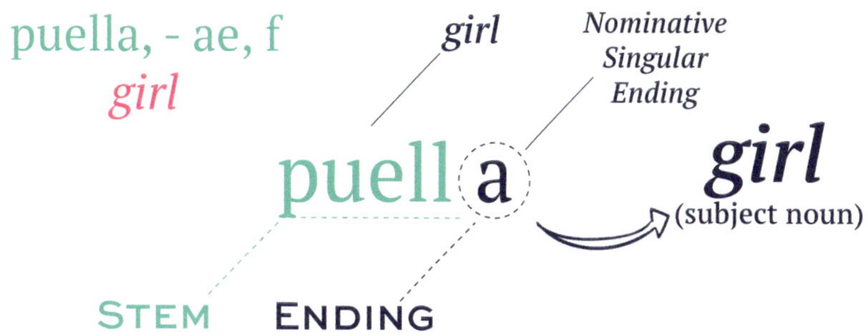

If we change the ending of *puella*, the use of the word changes, too, as below:

If the word *puellam* appeared in a sentence, it would have to be used as a direct object or as an object of a preposition. The word *puellam* may appear at the beginning of the sentence, in the middle, etc., but wherever it appeared, it would have to be translated as the direct object—that is, a noun that receives the action of the verb —or as an object of a preposition like *ad* or *in*.

The six cases we will cover include the **nominative** case, used for subjects, the **genitive** case, used to indicate possession, the **dative** case, used to refer to indirect objects, the **accusative** cases, used for direct objects, the **ablative** case, for objects of a preposition and prepositional phrases, and the **vocative** case, which is used for direct address (or when one noun speaks to another noun).

This particular concept requires a lot of practice, both in terms of memorizing the different endings, recognizing them, and knowing how they should be translated. This will take a lot of time, so be sure to practice every day and provide yourself with plenty of encouragement that you can do this.

A noun's endings also determine two other important ideas: gender and number. In Latin, the idea of **gender** corresponds to whether a noun can be classified as masculine, feminine, or neuter, a term that technically means "neither." The gender of a noun is normally pretty obvious, like the noun *puella*, meaning "girl," being feminine, or *puer*, meaning "boy," being masculine. We should note that most first declension nouns are feminine, including *puella* ("girl"), *aqua* ("water"), *via* ("way" or "road") and others.

But there are also first declension nouns that are masculine, not feminine. These nouns are typically jobs and professions such as *poeta* ("poet"), *nauta* ("sailor"), and *aurīga* ("chariot driver"), among others. Other times, the gender of a noun seems unconnected to its meaning, such as the masculine word *ager* for "field" or the neuter word *caelum* for "sky." The gender of a noun should be memorized along with its dictionary definition, with a letter like *m* or *f* for *masculine* or *feminine* being included on a flashcard or in your notes.

Number refers to whether the noun refers to one thing or a group of things—that is, one thing or two or more things. In Latin, the number is regarded as being either "singular" or "plural." In English, we typically add the letter *- s* or *- es* onto the end of a word to make it plural: the singular *table* becomes the plural *tables,* the singular *sandwich* becomes the plural *sandwiches*, and so on. Latin has a number of different ways that a singular noun may become plural, which we will learn over time and with much practice.

The ideas of case, number, and gender are all part of a noun's ending. That is, the last 1 to 4 letters of each noun will tell you the job the noun is doing in a sentence, whether that noun is singular or plural. The endings follow a particular pattern of endings called declension, of which there are five declensions in all. A **declension** is a pattern of endings, and a noun falls into and is assigned one out of the five total declensions.

One thing that provides much confusion is the **stem change** from the nominative singular to the genitive singular. In Latin, the nominative singular form of a noun is typically spelled one way, but when the noun appears in other cases, it has a slight spelling change (see diagram below).

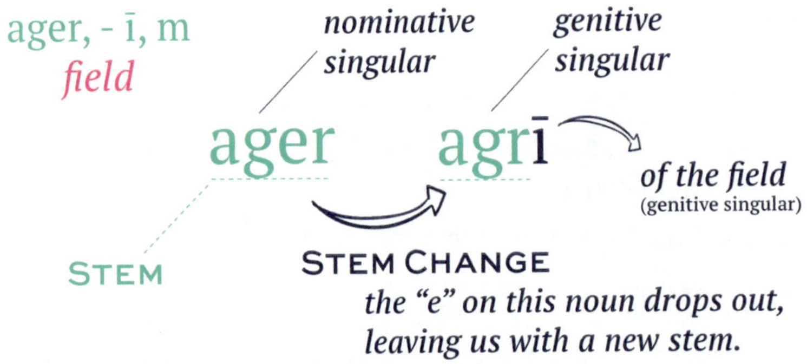

Vocabulary

Ablative Case
The ablative case is used to signify objects of a preposition.

Vocative Case
The case that indicates direct address, when one noun talks to or addresses another noun.

Gender
In Latin, nouns are further identified as belonging to any one of three genders that include masculine, feminine, or neuter.

Number
In Latin, the idea of *number* refers to a noun being either one thing or many things.

Declension
A declension is a pattern of endings, and a noun falls into any of five declensions.

Stem Change
The nominative singular form of a noun is different from its other case forms. As an example, *pater* is nominative singular, but the *e* drops out in the rest of the chart (example, *patris, patrī*, etc.) This process occurs in the third declension and in some second declension words.

In Latin, the "job" of a particular noun is not determined by its place in the sentence but by its case. We will be learning these cases for the next several chapters and covering them in greater detail.

Here are the six different cases plus the jobs they do in English, with the endings for the first declension feminine noun *puella, - ae, f.,* appearing below.

Singular Nouns / *The noun refers to only one person, place, or thing.*

Case	1st Declension Endings	1st Declension Sample Chart
Nominative Case *Subjects*	- a	puella / *a, the girl*
Genitive Case *Possession*	- ae	puellae / *of the girl*
Dative Case *Indirect Objects*	- ae	puellae / *to* or *for the girl*
Accusative Case *Direct Objects/Object of a Preposition*	- am	puellam *a / the girl*
Ablative Case *Object of a Preposition*	- ā	puellā / *by, with,* or *from the girl*
Vocative Case *Direct Address*	- a	puella / *oh, girl*

Plural Nouns / *The noun refers to two or more people, places, or things.*

Case	1st Declension Endings	1st Declension Sample Chart
Nominative Case *Subjects*	- ae	puellae / *a, the girls*
Genitive Case *Possession*	- ārum	puellārum / *of the girls*
Dative Case *Indirect Objects*	- īs	puellīs / *to* or *for the girls*
Accusative Case *Direct Objects/Object of a Preposition*	- ās	puellās *a / the girls*
Ablative Case *Object of a Preposition*	- īs	puellīs / *by, with, or from the girls*
Vocative Case *Direct Address*	- ae	puellae / *oh, girls*

Lesson Review Questions

1. What is a noun?

2. What is a *case*? (Hint: Use the word *job* in your answer.)

3. What is a *stem*?

4. What is an ending? Where do we find the endings in Latin?

5. A Latin noun can be any one of what two numbers?

Lesson Review Questions

6. A Latin noun can be any one of what three genders?

7. What is a *declension*?

8. What are the six cases? Write them in order from top to bottom.

9. What determines the meaning of a sentence in English? What determines the meaning of a sentence in Latin?

First Declension Nouns

Below is the chart for first declension nouns.

Singular Nouns / *The noun refers to only one person, place, or thing.*

Case	1st Declension Endings	1st Declension Sample Chart
Nominative Case *Subjects*	- a	puella / *a, the girl*
Genitive Case *Possession*	- ae	puellae / *of the girl*
Dative Case *Indirect Objects*	- ae	puellae / *to* or *for the girl*
Accusative Case *Direct Objects*	- am	puellam *a / the girl*
Ablative Case *Object of a Preposition*	- ā	puellā / *by, with,* or *from the girl*
Vocative Case *Direct Address*	- a	puella / *oh, girl*

Plural Nouns / *The noun refers to two (or more) people, places, or things.*

Case	1st Declension Endings	1st Declension Sample Chart
Nominative Case *Subjects*	- ae	puellae / *a, the girls*
Genitive Case *Possession*	- ārum	puellārum / *of the girls*
Dative Case *Indirect Objects*	- īs	puellīs / *to* or *for the girls*
Accusative Case *Direct Objects*	- ās	puellās *a / the girls*
Ablative Case *Object of a Preposition*	- īs	puellīs / *by, with, or from the girls*
Vocative Case *Direct Address*	- ae	puellāe / *oh, the girls*

Latin Nouns: First Declension

Instructions: All Latin nouns *decline*, meaning that they change their endings according to a set pattern. Please decline the following first declension nouns below.

Singular Nouns / *The noun refers to only one person, place, or thing.*

Case	1st Declension Feminine *puella, puellae*: girl	1st Declension Feminine *aqua, aquae*: water	1st Declension Feminine *lupa, lupae*: she-wolf
Nominative Case *Subjects*	puella		
Genitive Case *Possession*		aquae	
Dative Case *Indirect Objects*			lupae
Accusative Case *Direct Objects*			
Ablative Case *Object of a Preposition*			
Vocative Case *Direct Address*			

Plural Nouns / *The noun refers to two (or more) people, places, or things.*

Case	1st Declension Feminine *puella, puellae*: girl	1st Declension Feminine *aqua, aquae*: water	1st Declension Feminine *lupa, lupae*: she-wolf
Nominative Case *Subjects*			
Genitive Case *Possession*			
Dative Case *Indirect Objects*	puellīs		
Accusative Case *Direct Objects*		aquās	
Ablative Case *Object of a Preposition*			lupīs
Vocative Case *Direct Address*			

ACTIVITY

Latin Paradigms: Second Declensions

Below is the chart for second declension nouns.

Singular Nouns / *The noun refers to only one person, place, or thing.*

Case	2nd Declension Masculine	2nd Declension Masculine	2nd Declension Neuter
Nominative Case *Subjects*	puer / a, the boy	hortus / a, the garden	caelum / a, the heaven
Genitive Case *Possession*	puerī / of the boy	hortī / of the garden	caelī / of the heaven
Dative Case *Indirect Objects*	puerō / to *or* for the boy	hortō / to *or* for the garden	caelō / to *or* for heaven
Accusative Case *Direct Objects*	puerum / a, the boy	hortum / a, the garden	caelum / a, the heaven
Ablative Case *Object of a Preposition*	puerō / by, with, or from the boy	hortō / by, with, or from the garden	caelō / by, with, or from the heaven
Vocative Case *Direct Address*	puer / oh, boy	horte / oh, garden	caelum / oh, heaven

Plural Nouns / *The noun refers to two (or more) people, places, or things.*

Case	2nd Declension Masculine	2nd Declension Masculine	2nd Declension Neuter
Nominative Case *Subjects*	puerī / the boys	hortī / the gardens	caela / the heavens
Genitive Case *Possession*	puerōrum / of the boys	hortōrum / of the gar-dens	caelōrum / of the heav-ens
Dative Case *Indirect Objects*	puerīs / to *or* for the boys	hortīs / to *or* for the gardens	caelīs / to *or* for the heavens
Accusative Case *Direct Objects*	puerōs / the boys	hortōs / the gardens	caela / the heavens
Ablative Case *Object of a Preposition*	puerīs / by, with, or from the boys	hortīs / by, with, or from the gardens	caelīs / by, with, or from the heavens
Vocative Case *Direct Address*	puerī / oh, boys	hortī / oh, gardens	caela / oh, heavens

LATIN PARADIGMS

Latin Nouns: Second Declension

Instructions: All Latin nouns *decline*, meaning that they change their endings according to a set pattern. Please decline the following second declension nouns below.

Singular Nouns / *The noun refers to only one person, place, or thing.*

Case	2nd Declension Masculine *puer, puerī*: boy	2nd Declension Masculine *ager, agrī*: field	2nd Declension Neuter *caelum, caelī*: sky
Nominative Case *Subjects*	puer		
Genitive Case *Possession*		agrī	
Dative Case *Indirect Objects*			caelō
Accusative Case *Direct Objects*			
Ablative Case *Object of a Preposition*			
Vocative Case *Direct Address*			

Plural Nouns / *The noun refers to two (or more) people, places, or things.*

Case	2nd Declension Masculine *puer, puerī*: boy	2nd Declension Masculine *ager, agrī*: field	2nd Declension Neuter *caelum, caelī*: sky
Nominative Case *Subjects*			caela
Genitive Case *Possession*		agrōrum	
Dative Case *Indirect Objects*	puerīs		
Accusative Case *Direct Objects*			
Ablative Case *Object of a Preposition*			
Vocative Case *Direct Address*			

PARADIGM

Latin Paradigms: Third Declension

Below is the chart for third declension nouns.

Singular Nouns / *The noun refers to only one person, place, or thing.*

Case	3rd Declension Masculine	3rd Declension Feminine	3rd Declension Neuter	3rd Declension (i-stem)
Nominative Case *Subjects*	pater* / a, the father	māter* / a, the mother	nōmen* / a, the name	ars* / a, the art
Genitive Case *Possession*	patris / of the father	mātris / of the mother	nōminis / of the name	artis / of the art
Dative Case *Indirect Objects*	patrī / to *or* for the father	mātrī / to *or* for the mother	nōminī / to *or* for the name	artī / to *or* for the art
Accusative Case *Direct Objects*	patrem / a, the father	mātrem / a, the mother	nōmen / a, the name	artem / a, the art
Ablative Case *Object of a Preposition*	patre / by, with, or from the father	mātre / by, with, or from the mother	nōmine / by, with, or from the name	arte / by, with, or from the art
Vocative Case *Direct Address*	pater/ oh, father	māter / oh, mother	nōmen / oh, name	ars / oh, art

Plural Nouns / *The noun refers to two (or more) people, places, or things.*

Case	3rd Declension Masculine	3rd Declension Feminine	3rd Declension Neuter	3rd Declension (i-stem)
Nominative Case *Subjects*	patrēs / the fathers	mātrēs / the mothers	nōmina / the names	artēs / the arts
Genitive Case *Possession*	patrum / of the fathers	mātrum / of the mothers	nōminum / of the names	artium / of the arts
Dative Case *Indirect Objects*	patribus / to *or* for the fathers	mātribus / to *or* for the mothers	nōminibus / to *or* for the names	artibus / to *or* for the arts
Accusative Case *Direct Objects*	patrēs / the fathers	mātrēs / the mothers	nōmina / the names	artēs / the arts
Ablative Case *Object of a Preposition*	patribus/ by, with, or from the fathers	mātribus/ by, with, or from the mothers	nōminibus / by, with, or from the names	artibus/ by, with, or from the arts
Vocative Case *Direct Address*	patrēs/ oh, fathers	mātrēs/ oh, mothers	nōmina / oh, names	artēs/ oh, arts

**Please note that the nominative singular form for the third declension is irregular. The* e *has been marked in blue to signify this ending only appears in the nominative singular.*

LATIN PARADIGMS

Latin Nouns: Third Declension

Instructions: Please decline the following third declension nouns in the space provided.

Singular Nouns / *The noun refers to only one person, place, or thing.*

Case	3rd Declension Masculine *pater, patris*: father	3rd Declension Feminine *māter, mātris*: mother	3rd Declension Neuter *nōmen, - is*: name
Nominative Case *Subjects*			
Genitive Case *Possession*			
Dative Case *Indirect Objects*			nōminī
Accusative Case *Direct Objects*		mātrem	
Ablative Case *Object of a Preposition*	patre		
Vocative Case *Direct Address*			

Plural Nouns / *The noun refers to two (or more) people, places, or things.*

Case	3rd Declension Masculine *pater, patris*: father	3rd Declension Feminine *māter, mātris*: mother	3rd Declension Neuter *nōmen, - is*: name
Nominative Case *Subjects*			
Genitive Case *Possession*			
Dative Case *Indirect Objects*	patribus		
Accusative Case *Direct Objects*		mātrēs	
Ablative Case *Object of a Preposition*			nōminibus
Vocative Case *Direct Address*			

Verbs, Stems, & Endings

THE WORD IN LATIN for "word" is *verbum* and provides the root of our English word, **verb**. This connection demonstrates how the most important word in a Latin sentence is most often the verb. A verb can refer to an action or a state of being, what the subject is doing or being. The verb that tells what the subject is doing is known as an **action verb**, and English has two kinds of action verbs: **transitive verbs**, which take a direct object, and **intransitive verbs**, which do not. A **linking verb** is a word like *is* or *was* that refers to a state of being. For example, in the sentence, *The Romans are strong*, the word *are* is a linking verb joining together *The Romans* to the state of being *strong*.

In English, we also use **helping verbs**. Words like *had*, *will, shall, would,* or *should* all indicate when or how an action takes place, along with the main verb. Together, they form the verb phrase. But that is English. Latin is an inflected language, meaning that the last 1 to 4 letters of each Latin word determines how that word is used in a sentence. These crucial 1 to 4 letters at the end of each Latin word tell the reader who is doing the action of the verb, the time the action is being done (the **tense**) , and even the kind of action that it is, whether the action is ongoing, habitual, or completed (called the **aspect**). Often, we use the word **form** to refer to the particular "shape" that the verb takes in a particular context. The form of a verb can change its shape so that it is translated in a slightly different way.

Every verb is broken down like this into two parts: the stem (or root) and the ending. The **stem** (or root) is the part of the verb that does not change, while the **ending** is those last 1 to 4 letters that identify the time an action is taking place, who is doing it, and what kind of action it is. We can think of endings as an element that gives you information about who is doing the action of the verb, a kind of code we English speakers have to learn to decipher. In this way, each Latin word is like a puzzle piece, and the Latin sentence is the whole puzzle. We use the endings to help us figure out how the puzzle pieces fit together. Here's an example:

studeō, studēre*
to strive, to study, to be attached to

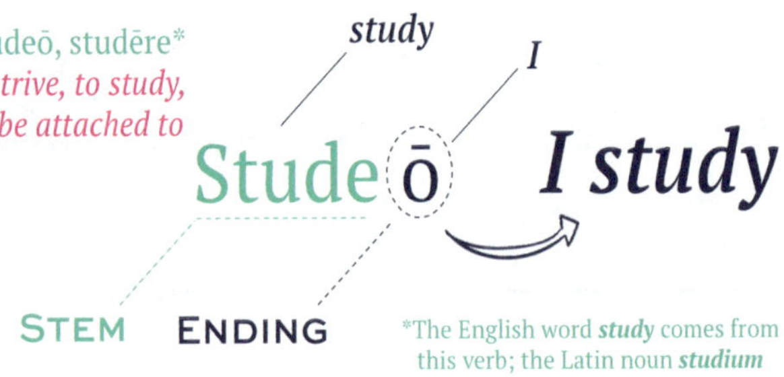

*The English word ***study*** comes from this verb; the Latin noun ***studium*** means "zeal" or "esteem."

BIG IDEA

A verb is a word that refers to an action or a state of being and, in Latin, is made up of two parts: its base (which does not change) and its endings, which changes to tell the reader information like the person (who is doing the action)*, the tense* (when it happens)*, and the number* (and how many people are doing the action) *of that verb.*

Vocabulary

Verb
A word that refers to an action or a state of being.

Action Verb
A word that tells what the subject is doing.

Transitive Verb
A verb that takes a direct object.

Intransitive Verb
A verb that does not take a direct object.

Linking Verb
A verb that joins together a subject and a subject complement (like an adjective or a noun).

Helping Verb
A word added to the main verb indicating a verb's tense, voice, aspect, or mood.

Tense
The time an action takes place.

Aspect
The kind of action taking place, which can be ongoing, completed, or habitual.

Form
The particular way or shape a verb appears as indicated by its base and its ending.

Stem
The part of the verb that does not change. Alternatively, we call this word the "root" or the "base" of the verb.

Ending
The last 1 to 4 letters that identify the time an action is taking place, who is doing it, and what kind of action it is.

In the diagram, we have the Latin verb ***studeō***; the stem (or the root) is *stude*, the ending is *ō*, and taken together, we have the verb ***studeō***, meaning "I study." But if we change the ending, we get a slightly different meaning.

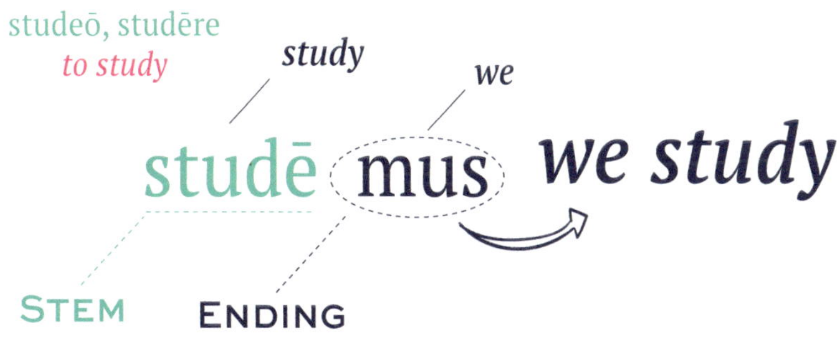

In the diagram above, we changed the ending so that we had a different group of people—represented by the pronoun *we*—doing the action of the verb. Here is another example:

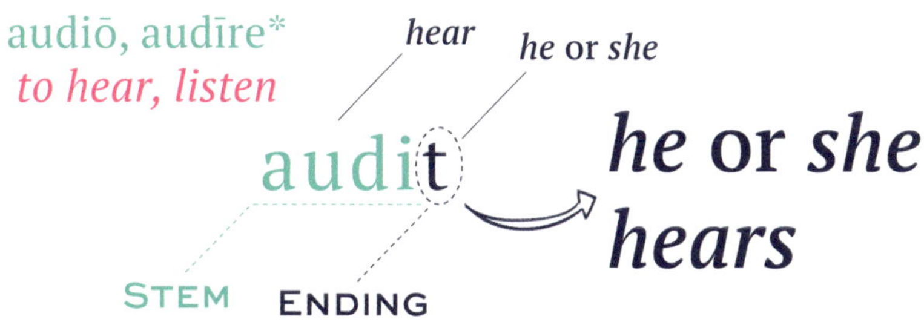

*The English word ***audience*** comes from this verb, a group of people who "listen."

And another:

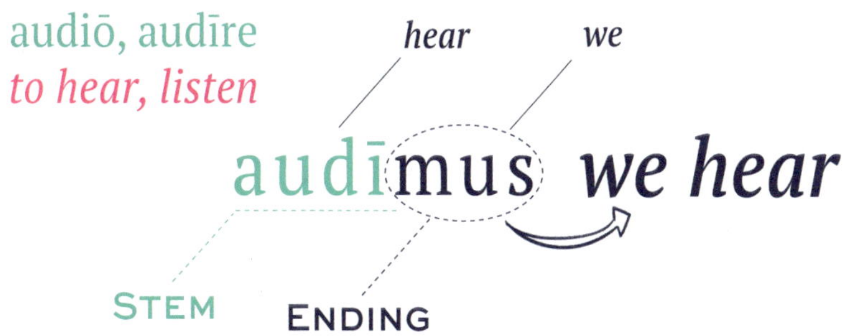

If you noticed the way each verb changed, part of the verb–the stem–did not change, and part of the verb–the ending–did change. When the endings changed, the pronouns we used to translate the verb also changed. The endings tell you certain information that, in English, is done by nouns, pronouns, and helping verbs placed in and around the main verb.

Taken together, the stem and the ending give us a Latin verb. Together, they give us the *form* of the verb that we see in a Latin text. We can think of form kind of like a shape in the same way dough can be shaped into many different things but still remain dough. A verb in Latin can take a few different shapes or forms depending on certain markers such as its person, number, and tense. Here is a breakdown of the information the ending of a verb conveys:

Person: The agent doing the action of a verb, which is typically a human being–hence, person–but could be any noun.

Tense: The time an action takes place.

Number: The number of things doing the action of the verb, whether singular or plural. If it is singular, then it is only one thing; if it is plural, it is two or more things.

Of these three, one of the most important (and trickiest) of these categories is person. The word *person* refers to the person, or group of people, or thing, or group of things, doing the action of the verb. The ending tells the reader what person–and thus what pronoun–to use when translating that verb. Latin has its own pronouns (like *ego* for "I" and *tu* for "you"), each of which declines according to its own chart. The verb endings tell the reader what person is doing the action of the verb and thus what pronoun to use in translating it.

And the idea of *tense* refers to the time an action takes place–in English, the tenses are the past, present, or future. Latin has six tenses, and each tense has its own endings and rules for translating them. Those tenses are as follows:

- The **present tense**, which indicates ongoing action happening at the present time
- The **imperfect tense**, for ongoing, repeated, and progressive actions happening in the past
- The **future tense**, for actions that will take place in the future
- The **perfect tense**, used for a completed action that occurred in the past
- The **pluperfect tense**, used for completed actions that occurred before another action in the sentence
- And the **future perfect tense**, for actions that will be completed in the future before another action takes place.

Each of the six tenses has its own endings and its own charts, and we will cover each of them in this book. These ideas seem difficult at first, but with practice and effort, we can commit them to mastery.

A·Z

Vocabulary

Person
The agent doing the action of a verb, which is typically a human being–hence, person–but could be any noun.

Number
The number of people, places, or things doing the action of a verb. A verb can *singular* (one) or *plural* (two or more).

Present Tense
The tense used for actions happening now, in the present time, which are ongoing and progressive actions (Example, *I am walking)*.

Imperfect Tense
The tense used for ongoing, habitual actions happening in the past (Example, *I was walking)*.

Future Tense
The tense used for actions that will occur in the future (Example, *I will walk)*.

Perfect Tense
The tense used for completed actions that occurred in the past (Example, *I walked)*.

Pluperfect Tense
The tense used for completed actions that occurred before another action in the past (Example, *I had walked)*.

Future Perfect Tense
The tense used for actions that will be completed before another action in the future (Example, *I will have walked)*.

Lesson Review Questions

1. What is a *verb*? What do verbs do in a sentence?

2. What is the difference between the *stem* of a verb and the *endings* of a verb?

3. In Latin, what does it mean that a verb has a *person*?

4. What are the six different tenses in Latin?

GUIDED NOTES

Latin Verbs

Instructions: In the space below, write a short description of the following elements of Latin verbs.

Term or Component	*Definition*
Verb	
Person	
Tense	
Number	
Infinitive	

ACTIVITY

Verbs Persons (in English)

Instructions: Read over each sentence and identify the person and number for each English verb. Write your answers in the space provided under each verb. Remember that by *number*, we mean "singular" or "plural."

Example: ***I study Latin*****:** 1st **Person, Singular**

1. We study many subjects.

_________ Person _________ Number

2. You (all) study Latin

_________ Person _________ Number

3. The Romans conquered the Mediterranean.

_________ Person _________ Number

4. You walk to the Forum.

_________ Person _________ Number

5. We walk to the gym.

_________ Person _________ Number

6. They walk to the gym.

_________ Person _________ Number

7. I walk to the gym.

_________ Person _________ Number

8. I read a good book.

_________ Person _________ Number

9. They read a good book.

_________ Person _________ Number

10. You (all) read a good book.

_________ Person _________ Number

11. We carry our books.

_________ Person _________ Number

12. You carry the chair.

_________ Person _________ Number

13. I carry my water bottle.

_________ Person _________ Number

14. He carries his backpack.

_________ Person _________ Number

ACTIVITY

Verbs Persons (in English)

Instructions: Continue the exercise from the previous page.

15. We walk around the park.

_________ Person _________ Number

16. Julius and I play baseball.

_________ Person _________ Number

17. You, mom, and dad should all read this book.

_________ Person _________ Number

18. Happiness is a life lived in accordance with virtue.

_________ Person _________ Number

19. Thales of Miletus was the first scientist.

_________ Person _________ Number

20. I finished my homework early.

_________ Person _________ Number

21. My brother and I played baseball in the backyard.

_________ Person _________ Number

22. You should go to bed at an early hour.

_________ Person _________ Number

23. June is named for Juno, the queen of the gods.

_________ Person _________ Number

24. I looked longingly at a cloud.

_________ Person _________ Number

25. The full moon was beautiful last night.

_________ Person _________ Number

26. He met a friend at the Forum.

_________ Person _________ Number

ACTIVITY

Verbs Persons (in English)

Instructions: Continue the exercise from the previous page.

27. The Via Appia ran from Rome to Brundisium.

________ Person ________ Number

28. They studied the works of Plato in class.

________ Person ________ Number

29. The Roman philosopher Seneca wrote tragic plays.

________ Person ________ Number

30. Augustus, Tiberius, Caligula, Claudius, and Nero were all members of the Julio-Claudian dynasty.

________ Person ________ Number

31. Tacitus was a historian famous for his book, the *Annals*.

________ Person ________ Number

32. You all should meet us at the Porta Capena.

________ Person ________ Number

33. It takes a lot of money to live in Corinth.

________ Person ________ Number

34. You (singular) should meet us at the Porta Capena.

________ Person ________ Number

35. Rome was not built in a day.

________ Person ________ Number

CHAPTER 3 / CAPITULUM III

Voice, Mood, & Principal Parts

SINCE WE SPEAK English as our first language, we do not often think about the concepts of voice or mood with verbs. They seem intuitive to us, but in Latin, we have to either form or recognize verbs in a particular voice or mood, which requires us to consider what these concepts mean and what they are composed of. In this chapter, we will review the ideas of voice and mood, as well as the important topic of principal parts. Let's begin with the concept of voice first.

In simplest terms, the term **voice** refers to who is doing the action of the verb in the sentence. In other words, voice refers to the relationship between the subject and the verb—is the subject *doing* the action, or is the action *being done* to the subject? We say that people can be active—getting outside and playing games—or be passive —staying indoors and allowing things to happen to you. In a similar way, there are two different voices: an active voice and a passive voice. We say that a verb is in the **active voice** if the subject is doing the action of the verb, as in the examples:

- *I carry a book.*
- *He throws the ball.*
- *The boy sees a wolf.*
- *We study Latin.*
- *You are playing a game.*

In each sentence, the subject performs whatever the action of the verb happens to be—playing, carrying, looking, studying, and so on. The term active voice derives from the Latin verb *ago, agere*, meaning "to do, drive, or lead." Whenever the subject is doing the action of the verb, the sentence is in the active voice.

In contrast, the term **passive voice** occurs whenever the action of the verb is being done to the subject.

- *The book is carried by me.*
- *The ball is thrown by him.*
- *A wolf is seen by the boy.*
- *Latin is studied by us.*
- *A game is played by us.*

In each of the sentences above, the subject is not actually doing anything. Instead, the action is being done to the subject. The term "passive" comes from the Latin

BIG IDEA

A verb has five aspects: the person (who's doing the action), the tense (when the action occurs), the number (how many people or things are doing the action), the voice (whether the action is being by the subject or done to the subject), and the mood (whether the action is happening, must happen, or could happen).

Vocabulary

Voice
The relationship between the verb and the person (or thing) completing the action of that verb.

Active Voice
The voice used when the subject is doing the action of the verb.

Passive Voice
The voice used when the subject is not doing the action of the verb; instead, another noun is receiving the action of the verb.

Mood
The attitude of the speaker to whatever action is being described in the sentence.

Indicative Mood
The indicative mood describes actions as they happen in the real world.

and Greek verb *patior, pati, passus sum*, meaning "to suffer" or "endure." The ancient world looked at suffering and hardship as something one endured but did not actually do—instead, it was all about withstanding something that happened to you.

In Latin, we have already seen how verbs are formed in the active voice. Indeed, active voice verbs are all we have seen. The passive voice in Latin is far more complicated than it is in English, and we will practice how to form the passive voice later in this chapter. For every chart you learn for active voice verbs, there is a whole other corresponding chart for verbs in the passive voice. For now, let's turn to the concept of mood for verbs.

Mood

Verbs, like people, can have moods. A person can be in a good mood, bad mood, happy mood, or sad mood, all of which describe the relationship between a person and their present circumstances. In a similar way, verbs have a **mood** that conveys the attitude of the speaker to whatever action is being described in the sentence. We have three moods across English and Latin: the indicative, imperative, and subjunctive. Let's look at each of these moods now and what they mean.

First, there's the indicative mood. The **indicative mood** is used to describe actions and events as they happen in the real world. The word *indicative* comes from the Latin word *dīcō, dīcere*, meaning "to speak" or "say," and refers to any plain statement about events happening in the world. Verbs in the indicative mood include the following:

- *I clean up my room.*
- *You are reading a book.*
- *She is walking to school.*
- *We are studying Latin.*
- *You all are preparing to go home.*
- *They are climbing a tree.*

Each sentence describes or speaks about some action going on in the real world at some indefinite point in time.

Second, there's the imperative mood. The **imperative mood** is used for commands or actions that must be completed. The word *imperative* comes from the Latin word *imperium*, meaning "the power to command" and is the root of our word for *emperor*. An imperative refers to any command, directive, or order, any kind of demand issued by the speaker. Some examples include:

- *Clean your room, please.*
- *Carry this book.*
- *Read this for homework.*

We should note that in the imperative mood, the pronoun *you* or *you (all)* is used as the implied subject. In each case, someone is being told to clean a room, carry a book, or complete some task the speaker considers important.

Commands in Latin are distinguished between a positive command—telling someone to do something—and negative commands—telling someone to *not* do something—as well as between commands given to one person or commands given to multiple people. **Positive commands** are formed from the infinitive form of a verb, as in the following diagram:

DIAGRAM 1
Imperative Mood Verbs
Positive Commands

For a command given to one person, remove the *-re* from the infinitive form and leave as is. For a command given to multiple people, remove the *-re* from the infinitive and add the letters *-te* onto the end of the verb.

A **negative command** follows a different process. In this, we base everything on the Latin irregular verb *nōlo, nōlle*, which means "to not want" or "not wish." In this case, the person issuing the command does not want the person to do such-and-such an action. We form the imperative from the verb *nōlo, nōlle*, which becomes *nōli* in the singular. If we are issuing a command to a group of people, we add the letters *-te* and use the plural form *nōlite* in the plural.

Then we add *nōlī* or *nōlīte* to the infinitive form of whatever action we do not want that person to do. If we commanded one person *not* to run, it would

Vocabulary

Imperative Mood
The mood used to issue commands.

Positive Command
A command telling someone to do something.

Negative Command
A command telling someone to *not* do something.

Subjunctive Mood
The mood used to indicate anything that could happen or should happen, generally referring to hypothetical scenarios.

Principal Parts
In Latin, each verb has four main forms that the verb can take.

First Principal Part
The first person, present tense form of a verb.

Second Principal Part
The infinitive form of a verb.

Third Principal Part
The first person, perfect tense form of a verb.

Fourth Principal Part
The perfect passive participle of a particular verb. Some verbs do not have a fourth principal part.

Participle
A verb that has been transformed into an adjective.

become *nōlī currere*. If we asked a group of people *not* to talk, it would become *nōlīte dicere*. Here is a diagram showcasing this change:

The Romans may have chosen *nōlō* because they struggled with the idea of telling someone to *not* do something. After all, actions are *volitional*, a word that comes from the Latin *volō, velle*, meaning "to wish" or "to want."

The third and final mood is the subjunctive mood. We use the **subjunctive mood** to indicate anything that could happen or should happen, any kind of hypothetical scenario or situation that has not actually happened but could.

In English, we form the subjunctive mood simply by adding a helping verb like *could*, *would*, or *should* next to a verb. These helping verbs indicate the idea of *potential,* things that could happen but have not happened yet.

To form the subjunctive mood in Latin is much more complicated. Like the passive voice, the Romans formed the subjunctive mood by changing the endings on a verb to indicate the verb was in the subjunctive, not the indicative, mood.

As a result, the subjunctive mood has its own charts for verbs in the present, imperfect, perfect, pluperfect, and future perfect tenses. Since these charts require considerable time to memorize, we will treat the charts for the subjunctive mood in its own chapter later in this book.

Principal Parts

If you look up a verb in the Latin dictionary, you'll find not one word but four different spellings of that particular Latin verb. For instance, you may see an entry like any of the following:

- *amō, amāre, amāvī, amatus:* to love
- *habeō, habēre, habuī, habitus:* to have
- *mittō, mittere, mīsī, mīssus:* to send
- *audiō, audīre, audīvī, audītus:* to hear

Each line contains one verb from each of the four conjugations, with each of its **four principal parts** written out in full. The principal parts are the four main ways that a verb can change its form depending on the time an action occurs, who is completing that action, and other important information communicated in the verb. There are four principal parts in all, which we can review one at a time.

The **first principal part** is the first person singular, present tense form of any verb. We have only covered the present tense forms of verbs, so this principal part should look familiar to you. The examples of the first principal part include *amō, habeō, mittō,* and *audiō*. See the diagram below:

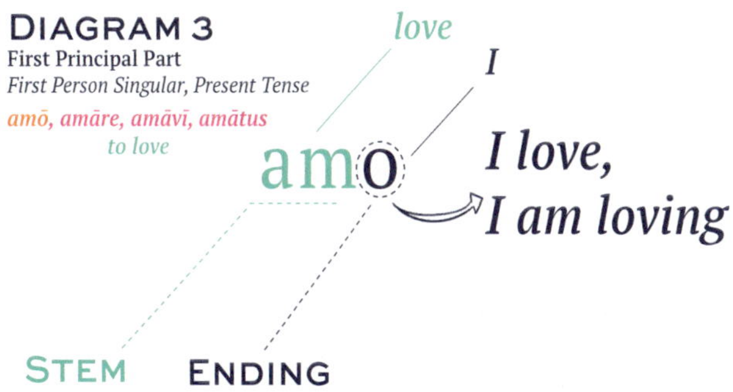

The **second principal part** is the infinitive form of that verb. We have dealt mostly with the first and second principal parts with verbs, so this should not cause you any trouble. The examples of the second principal part include *amāre, habēre, mittere,* and *audīre*.

The second principal part is particularly important because we use this part to identify the stem of a verb. Remember that the stem is the part of the verb that does not change. We find the stem by removing the letters *-re* at the end of the second principal part, leaving us with our stem.

The **third principal part** is the first person singular, perfect tense form of that verb. The perfect tense is used for an action completed in the past, and its stem is often very different from the present tense stem. We have not covered the perfect tense at this stage in our Latin journey, so this form will look new to you.

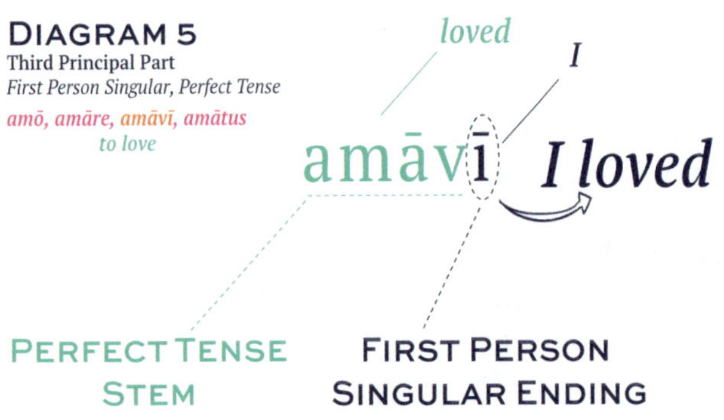

We will cover this tense in later chapters, but for now, examples of the third principal part include *portāvī, habuī, misī,* and *audīvī.* The diagram below breaks down the third principal part into its perfect tense stem and its personal ending.

The **fourth principal part** is the perfect passive participle. The fourth principal part is the most complicated of the four principal parts, so let's take the terms *perfect passive participle* and define them accordingly.

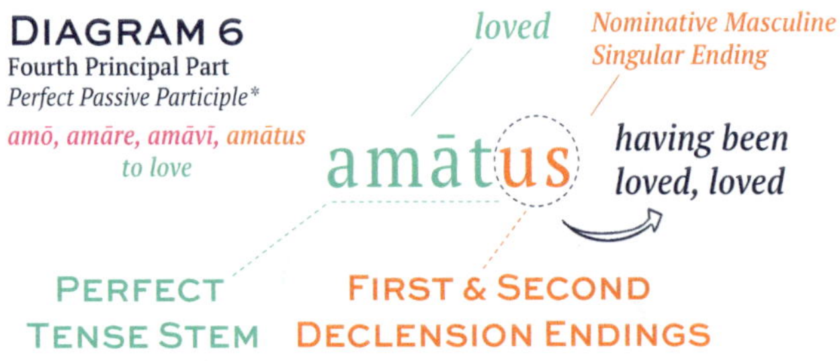

**A participle is an adjective formed from a verb (ex.* the loving parents*), and since they are adjectives, participles decline like adjectives, following the pattern of first and second declension adjectives.*

The term *perfect* comes from the perfect tense, meaning that the action of the verb is completed at some point in the past. The action is completed and finished and does not continue on into the present. One might of a sentence like, *I graduated from high school* as an example, for once you *graduate* from high school, the action is completed. One cannot go back and graduate from high school again.

The term *passive* comes from the passive voice, meaning that the action of the verb is being done to the subject. For example, a book is being carried, a game is being played, a subject is being studied, and so on.

And last, the term *participle* refers to a special kind of adjective made from a verb. A **participle** is part verb, part adjective, wherein a verb has been transformed into an adjective and modifies another noun the same way adjectives do. As some example, we could take the verb *talk* and transform it into the participle *talking* to modify a noun like *dog* or *cat—the talking dog, the talking cat.*

A perfect passive participle like *portatus, habitus, missus, audītus* is typically translated as the action "having been done" or simply adding the letters - *ed* onto the end of a verb. A participle like *missus* would be translated "having been sent" or even more simply, "sent"; a participle like *audītus* as "having been heard" or "heard," with other examples following this formula.

Participles can be tricky because they operate like adjectives. Since adjectives have to agree with the nouns they modify in case, number, and gender, likewise participles have to agree with the nouns they modify in case, number, and gender. Since participles are really adjectives, they have case endings similar to those of Latin adjectives in the first and second declensions.

For example, if we translated the phrase "the sent letter" into Latin, the phrase would be *epistula missa* , "the letter having been sent" or "the sent letter." We took the participle *missus* and removed the letters *-us* because that is actually an ending for a masculine singular noun.

We need to use *missa* to modify a feminine noun *epistula*, since *missa* has a feminine nominative singular ending, *-a*. That gives us *missa* and the *epistula missa,* "the sent letter."

The best way to learn the principal parts is to memorize them in and alongside new vocabulary. Take a few moments and write each of the four principal parts several times, enough times for you to internalize and memorize the changes that occur in each part.

When your teacher provides you with a list of new vocabulary words that include verbs, take a few moments to write down the principal parts a few times until these changes and forms become second nature to you.

The handout on the next page provides a diagram of each of the principal parts, plus some example verbs to help illustrate this concept.

BIG IDEA

Latin verbs are organized around four principal parts, the four different forms a verb can take. The first principal part is the first person singular, present tense form, the second is the active infinitive, the third is the first person singular, perfect tense form, and the last is the perfect passive participle.

LATIN DICTIONARY DEFINITION
VERBS DEEP DIVE

Latin dictionary definitions contain the information necessary to form the different inflections of a word.

What a verb looks like

amō, amāre, amāvī, amatus - to like, love
habeō, habēre, habuī, habitus - to have, hold
mittō, mittere, mīsī, missus - to send
audiō, audīre, audīvī, auditus - to hear, listen

PARTS OF A VERB

Infinitive

Perfect Passive Participle

amō, amāre, amāvī, amatus - to like, love

English meaning

1st Person Present Singular

1st Person Perfect Singular

FINDING A VERB'S STEM

1. Go to the infinitive / Second Principal Part
2. Remove the - *re*

FINDING A VERB'S CONJUGATION

1. Go to the Infinitive
2. Identify the ending

- *āre* → 1st Conjugation
- *ēre* → 2nd Conjugation
- *ere* → 3rd Conjugation
- *īre* → 4th Conjugation

Some verbs do not follow a regular, predictable pattern. We call these verbs ***irregular***.

Lesson Review Questions

1. What does it mean that a verb has a *voice*?

2. What is the *active voice*? What is it used for?

3. What is the *passive voice*? What is it used for?

4. What does it mean that a verb has a *mood*?

Lesson Review Questions

5. What is the *indicative mood*? What is it used for?

6. What is the *imperative mood*? What is it used for?

7. What is the *subjunctive mood*? What is it used for?

8. What are the *principal parts* of a verb?

Lesson Review Questions

9. What is the first principal part?

10. What is the second principal part?

11. What is the third principal part?

12. What is the fourth principal part? What exactly is a "participle"?

ACTIVITY / GRAMMAR PRACTICE

Identifying a Verb's Mood / In English

Instructions: Remember that the word *mood* refers to the kind of action a verb is expressing. The three moods include the *indicative mood*, which describes actions, the *imperative mood*, which expresses commands, and the *subjunctive mood*, which expresses commands that *could* happen or have the potential to happen. Read over each sentence and identify whether the mood of the verb is *indicative, imperative, or subjunctive.*

Example: *I love studying Latin.*

Indicative Imperative Subjunctive

(The sentence expresses a simple statement of fact.)

1. Romulus *founded* the city of Rome.

Indicative Imperative Subjunctive

2. March!

Indicative Imperative Subjunctive

3. Julius Caesar *could have reigned* for much longer than he did.

Indicative Imperative Subjunctive

4. The city of Rome *sits* on seven hills.

Indicative Imperative Subjunctive

5. Rome *could have been named* "Reme," had it been founded by Remus, the brother of Romulus.

Indicative Imperative Subjunctive

6. *Read* your homework.

Indicative Imperative Subjunctive

7. *Carry* that backpack.

Indicative Imperative Subjunctive

8. I *could go* to the Forum today.

Indicative Imperative Subjunctive

9. The Senate *met* on the Capitoline Hill.

Indicative Imperative Subjunctive

ACTIVITY / GRAMMAR PRACTICE

Identifying a Verb's Mood / In English

Instructions: Continue the exercise from the previous page.

10. The Senate *should be composed* only of seasoned, well-educated statesmen.

Indicative Imperative Subjunctive

11. I *bought* dormice, a Roman delicacy, at the market today.

Indicative Imperative Subjunctive

12. The Forum *was* the center of life in ancient Rome.

Indicative Imperative Subjunctive

13. *Hold up* your shield!

Indicative Imperative Subjunctive

14. The Romans *used* a shield called the *scūtum*, which they borrowed from the Samnites.

Indicative Imperative Subjunctive

15. We *should read* the *Aeneid* today.

Indicative Imperative Subjunctive

16. Romulus and Remus *should have died* on the banks of the Tiber River.

Indicative Imperative Subjunctive

17. A she-wolf *rescued* Romulus and Remus on the banks of the Tiber River.

Indicative Imperative Subjunctive

18. The Roman Empire *stretched* from Syria in the east to Spain in the west.

Indicative Imperative Subjunctive

19. *Memorize* these charts.

Indicative Imperative Subjunctive

20. The Roman Empire *could have endured*, had the Romans not lost sight of the path of wisdom and virtue.

Indicative Imperative Subjunctive

Active vs. Passive Voice / In English

Instructions: Read over each sentence and identify the voice of the verb written *in blue*. The verb will be either in the active voice or the passive voice. Remember that in the active voice, the subject is performing the action of the verb and in the passive voice, the action is being done to the subject.

First Example: **Romulus *founded* the city of Rome.**

(Active Voice) Passive Voice

Second Example: **The city of Rome *was founded* by Romulus.**

Active Voice (Passive Voice)

1. **The sacred geese *guard* the Temple of Juno.**

   Active Voice Passive Voice

2. **Tarquin Superbus *built* the Cloaca Maxima, a massive sewer running through Rome.**

   Active Voice Passive Voice

3. **The Tiber River *is flowing* through central Italy.**

   Active Voice Passive Voice

4. **The settlement on the Aventine Hill *was built* by Remus.**

   Active Voice Passive Voice

5. **Mount Vesuvius *erupted* in AD 79.**

   Active Voice Passive Voice

6. **The Circus Maximus *was built* by Tarquin Superbus.**

   Active Voice Passive Voice

7. **The Romans *conquered* the Italian peninsula over a period of five hundred years.**

   Active Voice Passive Voice

8. **Central Italy *was ruled* by a hill tribe called the Samnites.**

   Active Voice Passive Voice

9. **The scūtum *was adapted* by the Romans from the Samnites.**

   Active Voice Passive Voice

10. **The Romans *adapted* a shield from the Samnites called the *scutum*.**

    Active Voice Passive Voice

11. **Romulus *orchestrated* the abduction of the Sabines to find wives for his growing population of Roman citizens.**

    Active Voice Passive Voice

12. **The Roman Senate *was founded* by Romulus.**

    Active Voice Passive Voice

Active vs. Passive Voice / In English

Instructions: Continue the exercise from the previous page.

13. Remus *jumped* over the walls, which were built by Romulus.

Active Voice Passive Voice

14. The infants Romulus and Remus *were abandoned* on the banks of the Tiber River.

Active Voice Passive Voice

15. Gaius Scaevola *snuck* into the camp of Clusium, a city that was attacking Rome.

Active Voice Passive Voice

16. Roman religion *was founded* mostly by Numa Pompilius, Rome's second king.

Active Voice Passive Voice

17. The Romans *journeyed* to Athens to study the laws of the Athenians.

Active Voice Passive Voice

18. The walls on the Palatine Hill *were built* by Romulus.

Active Voice Passive Voice

19. Early in Roman history, the Romans *fought* in a *phalanx*, similar to that of the ancient Greeks.

Active Voice Passive Voice

20. The infants Romulus and Remus *were saved* by a she-wolf.

Active Voice Passive Voice

21. A she-wolf *saved* Romulus and Remus.

Active Voice Passive Voice

22. Lucretia *was knitting* socks for her husband, who was serving on the front lines of the Roman army.

Active Voice Passive Voice

23. Aeneas *went* from Troy to central Italy as part of the founding myth of Rome.

Active Voice Passive Voice

24. Dido *journeyed* to the city of Carthage, a wealthy trading hub in North Africa.

Active Voice Passive Voice

25. Aeneas' descendants *were cursed* by Queen Dido, angry and hurt that Aeneas had abandoned her.

Active Voice Passive Voice

26. Carthage *was founded* by exiles from the city of Tyre.

Active Voice Passive Voice

27. The bridge *was defended* by Horatius Cocles.

Active Voice Passive Voice

28. Famously, Rome *has* seven hills.

Active Voice Passive Voice

ACTIVITY / CHART PRACTICE

Finding the Stem & Identifying Conjugations

Instructions: Read over each entry, identify the stem of each verb and the conjugation of the verb. A sample entry has been provided for you.

Example: *portō, portāre, portāvī, portatus: to carry*

Stem: *port -*

Conjugation: *First Conjugation, based on its significant vowel, the ā, found in the second principal part.*

1. *audiō, audīre, audīvī, audītus*: to hear (like our English word *audience*)

Stem:____________________________

Conjugation: ____________________________

2. *amō, amāre,amāvī,amatus*: to love (like our English word *amor*)

Stem:____________________________

Conjugation: ____________________________

3. *doceō, docēre, docuī, doctus*: to teach (like our English word *doctrine*)

Stem:____________________________

Conjugation: ____________________________

4. *videō, vidēre, vīdī, vīsus*: to see (like our English word *video*)

Stem:____________________________

Conjugation: ____________________________

5. *tangō, tangere, tetigī, tāctum*: to touch

Stem:____________________________

Conjugation: ____________________________

ACTIVITY / CHART PRACTICE

Finding the Stem & Identifying Conjugations

Instructions: Continue the exercise from the previous page.

6. *veniō, venīre, vēnī, ventus*: to come

Stem:______________________________

Conjugation: ______________________________

7. *mittō, mittere, mīsī, missus*: to send (like our English word *mission*)

Stem:______________________________

Conjugation: ______________________________

8. *parō, parāre,parāvī,paratus*: to prepare

Stem:______________________________

Conjugation: ______________________________

9. *iubeō, iubēre, iussī, iussus*: to order

Stem:______________________________

Conjugation: ______________________________

10. *iaciō, iacere, iecī, iactus*: to throw

Stem:______________________________

Conjugation: ______________________________

11. *pōnō, pōnere, posuī, positus*: to place

Stem:______________________________

Conjugation: ______________________________

ACTIVITY / CHART PRACTICE

Finding the Stem & Identifying Conjugations

Instructions: Continue the exercise from the previous page.

12. *capiō, capere, cepī, captus*: to capture (like our English word *capture* or *captive*)

Stem:________________________________

Conjugation: __________________________

13. *habeō, habēre, habuī, habitus*: to have

Stem:________________________________

Conjugation: __________________________

15. *dīligō, dīligere, dīlēxī, dīlēctus*: to value (like our English word *diligent*)

Stem:________________________________

Conjugation: __________________________

16. *sentiō, sentīre, sēnsī, sēnsus*: to feel (like our English word *sense*)

Stem:________________________________

Conjugation: __________________________

17. *ambulō, ambulāre, ambulāvī, ambulātus*: to walk (like our English word *amble*)

Stem:________________________________

Conjugation: __________________________

18. *rapiō, rapere, rapuī, raptus*: to seize (like our English word *raptor*)

Stem:________________________________

Conjugation: __________________________

ACTIVITY / CHART PRACTICE

The Four Principal Parts

Instructions: Read over each entry and copy down the principal parts of that verb three times. Please make note of the macrons and where they appear.

1. *audiō, audīre, audīvī, audītus*: to hear

1st Time:

2nd Time:

3rd Time:

2. *portō, portāre, portāvī, portatus*: to carry

1st Time:

2nd Time:

3rd Time:

3. doceō, docēre, docuī, doctus: to teach

1st Time:

2nd Time:

3rd Time:

4. *mittō, mittere, mīsī, missus*: to send

1st Time:

2nd Time:

3rd Time:

Regular & Irregular Verbs

BOTH ENGLISH AND LATIN have regular verbs and irregular verbs. The word *regular* in **regular verbs** refers to a systematic, predictable pattern by which regular verbs change their form depending on the person completing that action or the time the action is completed. For instance, in English, the verb ***to walk*** is a regular verb because we simply add the letters -*ed* to make this verb past tense. See an example of this verb below:

Person & Number	Present Tense Verb Forms	Past Tense Verb Forms
1st Singular	I *walk*	I *walked*
2nd Singular	You *walk*	You *walked*
3rd Singular	He, she, it *walks*	He, she, it *walked*
1st Plural	We *walk*	We *walked*
2nd Plural	You (all) *walk*	You (all) *walked*
3rd Plural	They *walk*	They *walked*

In contrast, an **irregular verb** does not have a predictable, recognizable pattern by which it changes its forms depending on the time an action takes place. Verbs such as the verb ***to run*** and ***to go*** are irregular because their forms change depending on the time these actions take place. We have examples in English like the present tense ***I go*** versus the past tense ***I went***. The past tense form ***went*** came from a different verb with a present tense form ***wend***. The verb ***to go*** did not have a past tense form, so the past tense form of ***wend*** was used accordingly, giving us ***went*** in the past and ***go*** in the present.

The common irregular verb ***to be*** changes its spelling depending on the person doing the action of the verb, like below:

Person & Number	Verb Forms
1st Singular	I *am*
2nd Singular	You *are*
3rd Singular	He, she, it *is*
1st Plural	We *are*
2nd Plural	You (all) *are*
3rd Plural	They *are*

We say that the verb ***to be*** is irregular because it does not have a predictable pattern by which it changes its endings. Instead, those endings change frequently.

Latin operates in a very similar fashion with *regular* and *irregular* verbs. A regular verb has a recognizable,

BIG IDEA

A verb is regular *in that it conjugates, or changes its form, depending on the person doing the action or the time an action takes, according to a recognizable, predictable pattern. An irregular verb has no such pattern, so its forms must be memorized.*

New Vocabulary

Regular Verb
A regular verb changes its form according to a set, recognizable, predictable pattern.

Irregular Verb
An irregular verb does not have a predictable, recognizable pattern by which it changes its forms.

Review Vocabulary

Present Tense
The present tense refers to an ongoing, habitual action taking place at the present time.

1st Person Singular
If a verb ends with the letter *-o*, the verb is translated with the pronoun "I."

2nd Person Singular
If a verb ends with the letter *-s*, the verb is translated with the pronoun "you."

1st Person Plural
If a verb ends with the letters *-mus*, the verb is translated with the pronoun "we."

Infinitive
In Latin, an infinitive is a verbal noun, is translated with the word *to*, and ends with the letters *-re*. In English, an infinitive can be used as a noun, an adjective or an adverb.

predictable pattern by which its endings change, whereas an irregular verb may have up to six different forms of the verb in question. Consider the paradigm for the Latin verb ***sum, esse***:

Person & Number	Verb Forms
1st Singular	*sum* / I am
2nd Singular	*es* / You are
3rd Singular	*est* / He, she, it is
1st Plural	*sumus* / We are
2nd Plural	*estis* / You (all) are
3rd Plural	*sunt* / They are

Irregular Latin verbs tend to be more common in Latin. These verbs were used more frequently by the Romans, and so these irregular verbs had a greater opportunity for these words to change the more as people said them and used them. The more a word is used in everyday conversation, the more likely and more natural it is for that verb to change in one way or another.

As a result, the irregular forms seem especially confusing but also appear with higher frequency than other verbs. Some of the more common irregular verbs include:

Irregular Verbs	
sum, esse, fuī, futūrus to be	*nōlō, nōlle, nōluī* to not want
possum, posse, potuī to be able	*ferō, ferre, tulī, lātus* to bring, bear
eō, īre, iī / ivī, itus to go	edō, edere (ēsse), ēdī, ēsum to eat
volō, velle, voluī to wish, to want	mālō, mālle, māluī to prefer

Since these verbs are irregular, each of the verbs above conjugates in an unpredictable and wild fashion. Since you cannot predict what the verb will look like, you have to memorize them. The charts for these verbs appear on the following pages:

Person & Number	***mālō, mālle, māluī*** **to prefer, be unwilling**	***edō, ēsse, ēdī, ēsus*** **to eat**	***eō, īre, īvi, ītus*** **to go**
1st Singular	mālō / I prefer	edō / I eat	eō / I go
2nd Singular	māvīs / you prefer	edis *or* edēs / you do eat (Note the *ē* in *ēs*)	īs / you bring, go
3rd Singular	māvult / he, she, it wants	edit *or* edēs / he, she, it eats	īt / he, she, it goes
1st Plural	mālumus / we want	edimus / we eat	īmus / we go
2nd Plural	māvultis / you (all) want	editis *or* edēstis / you (all) eat	ītis / you (all) go
3rd Plural	mālunt / they want	edunt / they do not want	eunt / they go

Notice how we made the chart for ***eō, īre***. We took the infinitive ***īre*** and removed the letters ***re*** to give us the stem, - ***ī***. This verb is still irregular because it has special forms in the first person singular (***eō***) and third person plural (***eunt***). The verb appears as the words ***is*** and ***it*** , which look eerily similar to our English words "is" and "it," but knowing the rule makes this word easier to spot.

The chart for the verb ***edō, ēsse or edĕre*** (notice how ***ēsse*** has not only one but two possible infinitive forms), meaning "to eat," likewise looks eerily similar to the verb ***sum, esse.*** The macron over ***ēsse*** can be helpful for us modern Latin speakers, but the ancient Romans did not use macrons. To distinguish between ***edō, ēsse*** and ***sum, esse***, we have to rely on context clues in any Latin texts we are reading. Still, in memorizing this chart, carefully make note of the macrons, where they appear, and ***edō, ēsse*** should not cause you any trouble. Here are charts for other irregular verbs:

Person & Number	***volō, velle, voluī*** **to wish, want**	***nōlō, nōlle, nōluī*** **to not wish, not want**	***ferō, ferre, tulī, lātus*** ***to bring, bear***
1st Person Singular	volō / I want	nōlō / I do not want	ferō / I bring, I bear
2nd Person Singular	vīs / you want	nōn vīs / you do not want	fers / you bring, bear
3rd Person Singular	vult / he, she, it wants	nōn vult / he, she, it does not want	fert / he, she, it brings
1st Person Plural	volumus / we want	nōlumus / we do not want	ferimus / we want
2nd Person Plural	vultis / you (all) want	nōn vultis / you (all) do not want	fertis / you (all) want
3rd Person Plural	vōlunt / they want	nōlunt / they do not want	ferunt / they want

The key to learning and mastering irregular verbs is memorizing them. The task of memorizing so many different forms of so many different forms is quite difficult, so start small. Write out the principal parts of one verb until you commit them to mastery, beginning with more common verbs like *sum, esse* or *eō, īre* and adding more complicated verb forms like *mālō, mālle* and *ferō, ferre* over time. Do this at the beginning of class or during some downtime during the lesson; write one of the irregular verbs at the top of your home or on the margins of a test to help you remember these forms.

As you do this, you will find that it becomes easier to memorize not only verb forms but also complicated formulas or number sequences since, after all, your brain is a muscle—a fearfully and wonderfully made muscle, but still a muscle none the less. The more you work to develop this muscle, the more work that muscle will do.

Lesson Review Questions

1. What is a *regular* verb? What makes it "regular"?

2. What is an *irregular* verb? What makes it "irregular"?

Lesson Review Questions

3. Are *irregular* verbs more or less common than *regular* verbs?

4. How do you conjugate the irregular verb *eō, īre, īvi, ītus*? Please walk through the steps.

5. How do you conjugate the irregular verb *edō, ēsse or edĕre, ēdī, ēsum*? Please walk through the steps.

ACTIVITY

Irregular Latin Verbs

Instructions: Conjugate the verbs in the top row.

Person & Number	*sum, esse, fuī, futurus* to be	*possum, posse, potuī* to be able to, can
1st Person Singular	______________	______________
2nd Person Singular	______________	______________
3rd Person Singular	______________	______________
1st Person Plural	______________	______________
2nd Person Plural	______________	______________
3rd Person Plural	______________	______________

Person & Number	*vōlō, velle, vōluī* to wish, want	*nōlō, nōlle, nōluī* to wish, want
1st Person Singular	______________	______________
2nd Person Singular	______________	______________
3rd Person Singular	______________	______________
1st Person Plural	______________	______________
2nd Person Plural	______________	______________
3rd Person Plural	______________	______________

ACTIVITY

Irregular Latin Verbs

Instructions: Conjugate the verbs in the top row.

Person & Number	*edō, ēsse, ēdī, ēsum* to eat	*mālō, mālle, māluī* to prefer
1st Person Singular	____________	____________
2nd Person Singular	____________	____________
3rd Person Singular	____________	____________
1st Person Plural	____________	____________
2nd Person Plural	____________	____________
3rd Person Plural	____________	____________

Person & Number	*ferō, ferre, tulī, lātum* to bring, bear	*eō, īre, īvi, ītus* to go
1st Person Singular	____________	____________
2nd Person Singular	____________	____________
3rd Person Singular	____________	____________
1st Person Plural	____________	____________
2nd Person Plural	____________	____________
3rd Person Plural	____________	____________

ACTIVITY

Irregular Verbs (Latin & English)

Instructions: Read over each entry and supply the appropriate form of the verb *to be*. Identify the person and number for each entry in the space provided.

Example: *am*

Person & Number: *1st person, singular*

Translation: *I am*

1. are (English)

Person & Number: ____________________

Translation: ____________________

2. is (English)

Person & Number: ____________________

Translation: ____________________

3. sunt

Person & Number: ____________________

Translation: ____________________

4. possum

Person & Number: ____________________

Translation: ____________________

5. est

Person & Number: ____________________

Translation: ____________________

6. itis

Person & Number: ____________________

Translation: ____________________

7. estis

Person & Number: ____________________

Translation: ____________________

ACTIVITY

Irregular Verbs (Latin & English)

Instructions: Continue the exercise from the previous page.

8. es

Person & Number: ______________________

Translation: ______________________

9. īmus

Person & Number: ______________________

Translation: ______________________

10. editis / edēstis

Person & Number: ______________________

Translation: ______________________

11. nōn vultis

Person & Number: ______________________

Translation: ______________________

12. volō

Person & Number: ______________________

Translation: ______________________

13. nōlumus

Person & Number: ______________________

Translation: ______________________

14. possunt

Person & Number: ______________________

Translation: ______________________

15. vīs

Person & Number: ______________________

Translation: ______________________

ACTIVITY

Irregular Verbs (Latin & English)

Instructions: Continue the exercise from the previous page.

16. īs

Person & Number: ______________________

Translation: ___________________________

17. māvult

Person & Number: ______________________

Translation: ___________________________

18. edis / edēs

Person & Number: ______________________

Translation: ___________________________

19. vult

Person & Number: ______________________

Translation: ___________________________

20. mālunt

Person & Number: ______________________

Translation: ___________________________

21. eō

Person & Number: ______________________

Translation: ___________________________

22. edunt

Person & Number: ______________________

Translation: ___________________________

23. it

Person & Number: ______________________

Translation: ___________________________

ROMAN FORUM

Photo by Nicole Reyes (Unsplash)

Section II

Verb Tenses

CHAPTERS

CHAPTER 5 / CAPITULUM V

The Present Tense & Verb Persons

FOR MOST OF this year, we will use the present tense. The word **tense** refers to when an action takes place. The way the action takes place, whether that action is completed, ongoing, or habitual, we call **aspect**. In Latin, the **present tense** refers to an ongoing, habitual action taking place at the present time. We translate a present tense verb as if the action of the verb is happening in the present, almost at the very moment you are reading the sentence on the page. Depending on context, we can supply a helping verb like *is* or *are* to signify the action as ongoing.

The Latin present tense is similar to the English **present progressive tense** (an ongoing action happening at the present time, as in *I am doing*) and the **simple present** (an action in the present that happens one time, as in *I do*). In translating Latin, we may use the present progressive or the simple present tense depending on context.

Latin being an inflected language, the endings tell you almost everything you need to know to translate the word. The present tense endings are as follows:

Ending	Person & Number
-*ō*	1st Person, Singular
-*s*	2nd Person, Singular
-*t*	3rd Person, Singular
-*mus*	1st Person, Plural
-*tis*	2nd Person, Plural
-*nt*	3rd Person, Plural

The present tense is the simplest form of a Latin verb, so that Latin students need only keep track of the stem (the meaning of the word itself) and the personal endings (who is doing the action).

If a verb ends with *o*, it is translated with the pronoun *I*. In certain tenses, a first person verb may end with *m*, but you do not have to worry about that right now. For instance, the verb *amō* means "I love," *habeō*, "I have," *mittō,* "I send," and *audiō,* "I hear." We call verbs that end with -*o* **first person singular**. With first person verbs, the person speaking is the one doing the action.

BIG IDEA

The present tense refers to an ongoing action that takes place at the present time; in translating the present tense, we use the meaning of the verb, the appropriate subject pronoun, and a helping verb like is *or* was *to show if the action is ongoing or not. Examples include "I love," "I do love," and "I am loving."*

Review Vocabulary

Tense
The time an action takes place.

New Vocabulary

Aspect
The way an action takes place and whether the action is ongoing, completed, or habitual.

Present Tense
In Latin, the term present tense refers to an ongoing, habitual action taking place at the present time.

Present Progressive Tense
In English, the present progressive tense refers to an ongoing, habitual action taking place at the present time.

Simple Present Tense
In English, the simple present tense refers to an action that happens in the present time and is completed.

First (or 1st) Person Singular
If a verb ends with the letter *-o*, the verb is translated with the pronoun "I."

Second (or 2nd) Person Singular
If a verb ends with the letter *-s*, the verb is translated with the pronoun "you."

First (or 1st) Person Plural
If a verb ends with the letters *-mus*, the verb is translated with the pronoun "we."

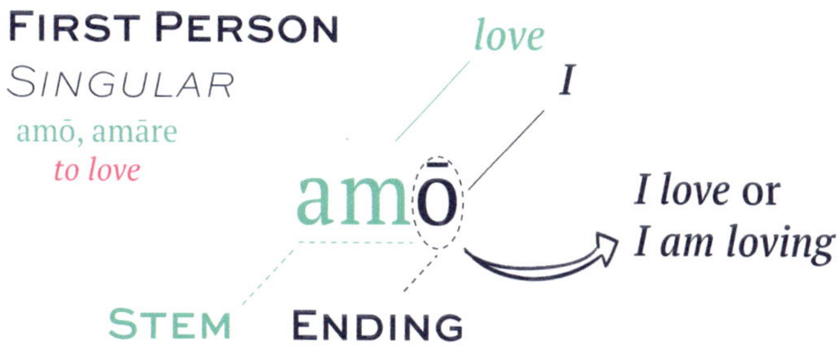

If a verb ends with the letter *-s*, then we use the pronoun *you*. Some examples include the verbs *amās*, "you love," *habēs*, "you have," *mittis*, "you send," and *audīs*, "you hear." We call verbs that end with *- s* **second person singular**. With second person verbs, the person doing the action is being spoken to.

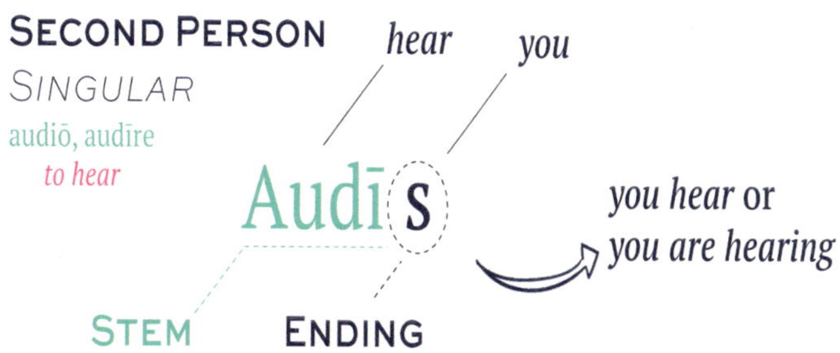

If a verb ends with the letter *-t*, one can use the pronouns *he*, *she*, or *it*. For instance, one can translate the verb *amat* with *he*, *she*, or *it loves* depending on the context of the sentence. If the sentence has a subject-noun, then you don't have to use a pronoun at all. Just use the subject-noun in the sentence—i.e., the noun doing the action of the verb. We call verbs with this *- t* ending **third person singular**. With third-person verbs, the person is being spoken about.

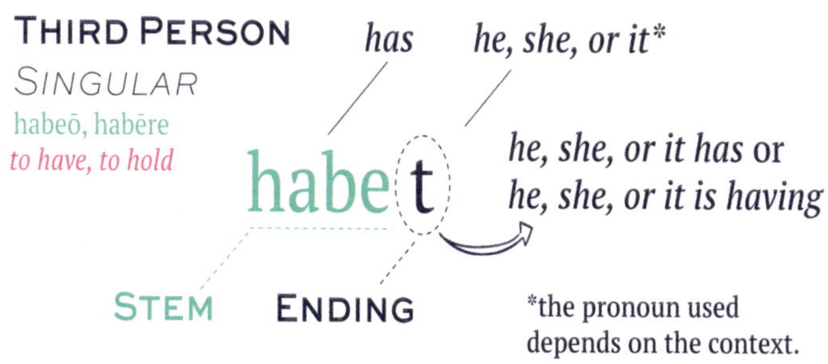

The above endings are with singular—that is, one person, place, or thing doing the action of the verb.

Next are the plural endings, which look similar. If a verb ends with *-mus*, it is translated with the pronoun *we*. Consider the verbs *amāmus*, mean ing "we love" or *habēmus*, meaning "we have." Verbs that end in - *mus* are **first person plural**.

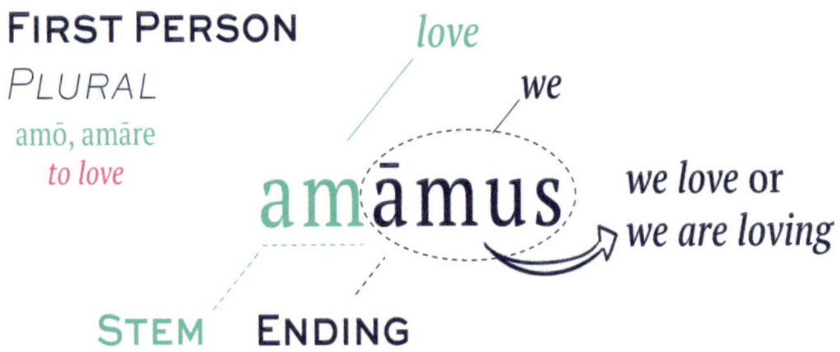

With -*tis*, we use the pronouns *you (implied plural)*, *you (all)*, or *y'all*. Consider the verbs *amātis*, meaning "you (all) love" or *habētis*, "y'all have." Verbs that end in - *tis* are called **second person plural**.

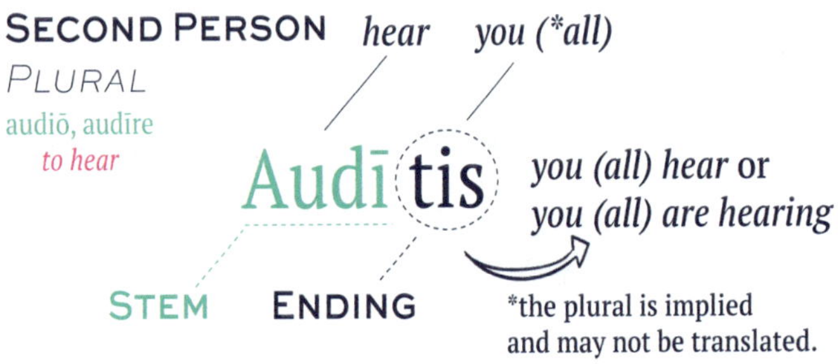

Lastly, if a verb ends with -*nt*; we can use the pronoun *they* as in the verbs *amant*, meaning "they love," or *habent*, meaning "they have." As with the third person singular, if the sentence has a subject-noun, then you don't have to use a pronoun at all. Just use that subject-noun—i.e., the noun doing the action of the verb.

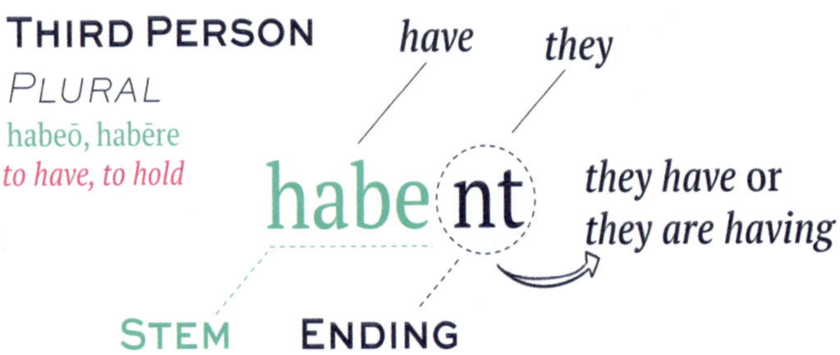

The endings -*o*, -*s*, -*t*, -*mus*, -*tis*, -*nt* should be memorized since they are the building blocks of the Latin verb system. To do so, say the endings out loud and write them out by hand as much as possible. Stems can change, so it is helpful to memorize the endings by writing out a particular verb and its chart in full. In total, these endings form the chart for the present tense appears at the top of the following page:

New Vocabulary

Second (or 2nd) Person Plural

If a verb ends with the letters -*tis*, the verb is translated with the pronoun "you" or "you (all)."

Third (or 3rd) Person Singular

If a verb ends with the letter -*t*, the verb is translated with the pronoun "he" or "she," or the subject-noun in the sentence.

Third (or 3rd) Person Plural

If a verb ends with the letters -*nt*, the verb is translated with the pronoun "they," or the subject-noun in the sentence.

Person & Number	*amō, amāre*: to love	*habeō, habēre*: to have	*mittō, mittere*: to send	*audiō, audīre*: to hear
1st Person, Sing	amō / I love	habeō / I have	mittō / I send	audiō / I hear
2nd Person, Sing.	amās / you love	habēs / you have	mittis / you send	audīs / you hear
3rd Person, Sing.	amat / he, she, it loves	habet / he, she, it has	mittit / he, she, it sends	audit / he, she, it hears
1st Person, Plural	amāmus / we love	habēmus / we have	mittimus / we send	audīmus / we hear
2nd Person, Plural	amātis/ you (all) love	habētis / you (all) have	mittitis/ you (all) send	audītis/ you (all) hear
3rd Person, Plural	amant / they love	habent / they have	mitt*unt* / they send	audiunt / they hear

The idea of "1st," "2nd," or "3rd" person can be quite confusing at first. Think, though, of the different kinds of narrators in a story. A story may have a "first-person narrator": in that case, the person telling the story is also a character in the story. A first person verb has the person doing the action also describing the action.

The same thinking also applies to verbs that are first person plural, except that the narrator is part of a larger group. When I say, "we will love Latin," I am referring to an action that the group and I will do together. We might describe these actions as the subjects both performing the action of the verb and describing that action.

Second person verbs can be a bit trickier. For second person singular and plural, the person (or people) doing the action of the verb is the person (or people) being addressed. If a teacher tells *you*, *you are a great student*, *you* are the subject of the linking verb *are*, but the person speaking is the *teacher*, not *you*. We might speak of the subject "being spoken to." In this case, we use the pronoun *you* to perform the action of the verb. The form looks similar for the second-person plural. But plural, second person verbs are trickier to translate because it is often an *implied plural*. In English, when we address a group of people, we can use the pronoun *you* and it is understood that it is a larger group than simply one individual. Accordingly, you may see second-person verbs translated as "*you*," "*you all*," "*you* (implied plural)," or the shortened " *y'all*."

A verb in the third person singular has the person describing an action he or she is not a part of. Think of a story with a "third-person narrator": in that case, the person telling the story is not a character in the story. The narrator is an entirely separate character and is not part of the action of the story. In this case, the subject is being spoken about.

The same thinking also applies to verbs that are third person plural, except that it is two or more people (or things) doing the action of the verb. The third-person becomes tricky, though, if the sentence has a subject in it. Then the subject of the sentence completes the action of the verb. If there is no subject, we supply the pronouns *he, she*, or *it* for a singular verb and the pronoun *they* for a plural verb.

To review, the term *tense* refers to the time an action takes place, and the term aspect refers to the kind of action it is. An action can take place in the present time, the past, or the future, and the action can be ongoing, completed, or habitual.

The Latin present tense refers to an action that takes place in the present time and is ongoing, and it is similar to the present progressive tense and simple present tense in English.

To translate the present tense, we find the meaning of the word, identify its personal endings, and describe the action as if it is taking place at the same time you, as the student, are reading it. These forms may seem confusing, but with practice they can be learned to mastery. So let's get going! *Bona fortuna*! (Good luck!)

Lesson Review Questions

1. In Latin, what does it mean that a verb has a *tense*?

2. What does it mean that a verb has a *number*?

Lesson Review Questions

3. What is the *present tense?*

4. How do you translate a verb that is in the *first person singular*? *First person plural?*

5. How do you translate a verb that is in the *second person singular*? *Second person plural?*

5. How do you translate a verb that is in the *third person singular*? *Third person plural?*

Latin Dictionary Definition
Verbs Deep Dive

Latin dictionary definitions contain the information necessary to form the different inflections of a word.

What a verb looks like

amō, amāre, amāvī, amatus - to like, love
habeō, habēre, habuī, habitus - to have, hold
mittō, mittere, mīsī, missus - to send
audiō, audīre, audīvī, auditus - to hear, listen

Parts of a Verb

Infinitive

Perfect Passive Participle

amō, amāre, amāvī, amatus - to like, love

English meaning

1st Person Present Singular

1st Person Perfect Singular

Finding a Verb's Stem

1. Go to the infinitive / Second Principal Part
2. Remove the - *re*

Finding a Verb's Conjugation

1. Go to the Infinitive
2. Identify the ending

- *āre* → 1st Conjugation
- *ēre* → 2nd Conjugation
- *ere* → 3rd Conjugation
- *īre* → 4th Conjugation

Some verbs do not follow a regular, predictable pattern. We call these verbs ***irregular***.

Latin Charts: The Present Tense & Verb Persons

Instructions: Below are charts for verbs in the present tense.

Person & Number	amō, amāre: to love	habeō, habēre: to have	mittō, mittere: to send	audiō, audīre: to hear
Present Tense / *The verb refers to an action currently occurring and is ongoing.*				
1st Person, Singular / *I*	amō / I love	habeō / I have	mittō / I send	audiō / I hear
2nd Person, Singular / *you*	amās / you love	habēs / you have	mittis / you send	audīs / you hear
3rd Person, Singular / *he, she, it*	amāt / he, she, it loves	habet / he, she, it has	mittit / he, she, it sends	audit / he, she, it hears
1st Person, Plural / *we*	amāmus / we love	habēmus / we have	mittimus / we send	audīmus / we hear
2nd Person, Plural / *you (impl. pl.)*	amātis/ you (all) love	habētis / you (all) have	mittitis/ you (all) send	audītis/ you (all) hear
3rd Person, Plural / *they*	amant / they love	habent / they have	mitt*unt* / they send	audiunt / they hear

Latin Charts: The Present Tense & Verb Persons

Instructions: Please conjugate the present tense of the following verbs, then translate. Please refer to the endings from the previous page.

Conjugate & Translate *parō, pārāre*: to prepare

Conjugation: ______________________

Singular

1st Singular: ______________________

Translation: ______________________

2nd Singular: ______________________

Translation: ______________________

3rd Singular: ______________________

Translation: ______________________

Plural

1st Plural: ______________________

Translation: ______________________

2nd Plural: ______________________

Translation: ______________________

3rd Plural: ______________________

Translation: ______________________

Conjugate and Translate *moveō, movēre, to move*

Conjugation: ______________________

Singular

1st Singular: ______________________

Translation: ______________________

2nd Singular: ______________________

Translation: ______________________

3rd Singular: ______________________

Translation: ______________________

Plural

1st Plural: ______________________

Translation: ______________________

2nd Plural: ______________________

Translation: ______________________

3rd Plural: ______________________

Translation: ______________________

The Present Tense / Practice

Instructions: Please conjugate the present tense of the following verbs, then translate.

Conjugate & Translate *iaciō, iacere*: to throw

Conjugation: ______________________

Singular

1st Singular: ______________________

Translation: ______________________

2nd Singular: ______________________

Translation: ______________________

3rd Singular: ______________________

Translation: ______________________

Plural

1st Plural: ______________________

Translation: ______________________

2nd Plural: ______________________

Translation: ______________________

3rd Plural: ______________________

Translation: ______________________

Conjugate and Translate *veniō, venīre, to come*

Conjugation: ______________________

Singular

1st Singular: ______________________

Translation: ______________________

2nd Singular: ______________________

Translation: ______________________

3rd Singular: ______________________

Translation: ______________________

Plural

1st Plural: ______________________

Translation: ______________________

2nd Plural: ______________________

Translation: ______________________

3rd Plural: ______________________

Translation: ______________________

ACTIVITY

The Present Tense & Verb Persons

Vocabulary Word / Meaning
legere: to read
studēre: to study
ambulāre / to walk

Instructions: Identify the person and number for each Latin verb. Write your answers in the space provided under each verb. Note, too, that most of these verbs can stand on their own in a sentence. For these first few exercises, the base is in green, while the ending is italicized and in *blue*. Translate the verb.

Example: *Studeō*: I study.

1. studē*mus*

Translation: ______________________________

2. studē*tis*

Translation: ______________________________

3. studē*re*

Translation: ______________________________

4. stude*nt*

Translation: ______________________________

5. ambulā*tis*

Translation: ______________________________

6. ambulā*s*

Translation: ______________________________

7. ambulā*re*

Translation: ______________________________

8. ambul*ō*

Translation: ______________________________

9. leg*ō*

Translation: ______________________________

10. legu*nt*

Translation: ______________________________

11. legi*tis*

Translation: ______________________________

12. lege*re*

Translation: ______________________________

13. legi*mus*

ACTIVITY

The Present Tense & Verb Persons

Vocabulary Word / Meaning
discere: to learn
audīre: to hear
portāre: to carry
pōtāre: to drink

Instructions: Continue the exercise from the previous page.

Translation: ______________________

14. legi***s***

Translation: ______________________

14. disci***s***

Translation: ______________________

15. disci***tis***

Translation: ______________________

16. pōtā***s***

Translation: ______________________

7. pōta***t***

Translation: ______________________

18. pōta***nt***

Translation: ______________________

19. audi***ō***

Translation: ______________________

20. portā***s***

Translation: ______________________

21. disc***ō***

Translation: ______________________

22. pōt***ō***

Translation: ______________________

23. pōtā***mus***

Translation: ______________________

24. portā***tis***

Translation: ______________________

The Imperfect Tense

RECALL THAT A verb refers to an action or a state of being. Accordingly, we speak of who is doing the action (the person), and how many people or things are doing that action (the number). We also speak of the time the action occurs (the **tense**) and of the kind of action it is, whether it is a completed action or if it is still occurring (the **aspect**). You can think of the time an action takes place as related to when you are reading it. Did the event take place as you are reading the sentence, before you read the sentence, or will it take place in the future?

In English, the **past progressive tense** is used for going, progressive, or habitual actions taking place the past. The past progressive tense is marked by a helping verb like *was* or *were*, plus the participial form of the verb, as in *I was going to the Forum yesterday* or *They were working in the garden*. The English past progressive tense is very similar to the Latin **imperfect tense**, although the Latin imperfect tense covers more actions than the English past progressive tense. This kind of action can be translated as an ongoing action ("was doing"), a habitual action ("used to do"), or a repeated action ("kept doing").

The imperfect tense may be the easiest tense to identify thanks to its tense markers. These **tense markers** are letters added to the base of the verb before its personal endings. The letters *-ba* serve as the tense markers in the imperfect. Whenever you see the letters *-ba* between the base of a verb and its personal endings, you should recognize that verb as being in the imperfect tense. Often, teachers call these markers the "imperfect sheep" since it looks like the sound a sheep makes—*ba*.

Here's an example of the imperfect tense, formed from the verb ***parābam***:

BIG IDEA

The imperfect tense describes ongoing or habitual actions taking place in the past; the action is not "complete" and thus not "perfect." In Latin, the letters ba *signal the imperfect tense and can be found between the verb's stem and personal endings. The imperfect tense can be translated as an ongoing action ("was doing"), a habitual action ("used to do"), or a repeated action ("kept doing").*

A·Z

Vocabulary

Verb
A word that refers to an action or a state of being.

Tense
The time an action takes, whether in the past, present, or future.

Aspect
The way an action takes place and whether the action is ongoing, completed, or habitual.

Past Progressive Tense
In English, this tense refers to an ongoing (or progressive) action that started in the past.

Tense Markers
Letters between the *base* of a verb and its personal endings indicating the tense of that verb.

Imperfect Tense
The imperfect tense refers to an ongoing, habitual action in the past.

The stem is from ***parāre,*** meaning "to prepare," and the personal ending is ***-m,*** which means we use the pronoun ***I*** to translate it. The presence of the tense markers ***-ba*** means the verb is in the imperfect tense, so we translate the verb ***parābam*** "I was preparing." Let's look at one more example, ***discēbāmus***, below:

The stem is from ***discere,*** meaning " to learn," and the personal ending is the first-person plural ending ***-mus,*** which means we use the pronoun ***we*** to translate it. The presence of the tense markers ***-ba*** means the verb is in the imperfect tense, so we translate the verb ***discēbāmus,*** "We were learning."

For good measure, let's consider one more example, formed from the verb ***trahō, trahere,*** meaning "to drag." If we wanted to say, "You were dragging," the word would be ***trahēbās*** in the singular and ***trahēbātis*** in the plural. The diagram for these ***trahēbās*** would look like this:

And for the second person plural ***trahēbātis***:

In the diagrams above, the only thing that changed is the personal endings, and so in our translations, the only thing that changes is the pronoun we use to translate that word. The imperfect tense requires practice and effort but can be learned to mastery. Let's begin memorizing it now.

Lesson Review Questions

1. What is a verb?

2. What is a verb tense? What does the idea of tense mean?

3. What is a "tense marker"?

4. What is the imperfect tense, and how do we identify the imperfect tense?

5. How should we translate the imperfect tense?

The Imperfect Tense / Practice

Instructions: Please conjugate the following verbs in the space below.

Imperfect Tense / *The verb refers to an action that began in the* **past** *but continues into the* **present**.

	1st Conjugation *amō, amāre: to love*	2nd Conjugation *moveō, movēre: to move*
1st Person / Singular	amābam / I was loving, kept loving, used to love	movēbam / I was moving, kept moving, used to move
2nd Person / Singular	amābās / you were loving, kept loving, used to love	movēbās / you were moving, kept moving, used to move
3rd Person / Singular	amābat / he, she, it was loving, kept loving, used to love	movēbat / he, she, it was moving, kept moving, used to move
1st Person / Plural	amābāmus / we were loving, kept loving, used to love	movēbāmus / we were moving, kept moving, used to move
2nd Person / Plural	amābātis / you (all) were loving, kept loving, used to love	movēbātis / you (all) were moving, kept moving, used to move
3rd Person / Plural	amābant / they were loving, kept loving, used to love	movēbant / they were moving, kept moving, used to move

Person & Number	1st Conjugation *putō, putāre: to think*	2nd Conjugation *teneō, tenēre: to hold*
1st Person, Singular	______	______
2nd Person, Singular	______	______
3rd Person, Singular	______	______
1st Person, Plural	______	______
2nd Person, Plural	______	______
3rd Person, Plural	______	______

The Imperfect Tense / Practice

Instructions: Please provide the charts for the following verbs in the space below.

Imperfect Tense / *The verb refers to an action that began in the* **past** *but continues into the* **present**.

Person & Number	3rd Conjugation *mittō, mittere, mīsī, missus:* to send	4th Conjugation *audiō, audīre, audīvī, audītus:* to hear
1st Person, Singular	mittēbam / I was sending, kept sending, used to send	audiēbam / I was hearing, kept hearing, used to hear
2nd Person, Singular	mittēbās / you were sending, kept sending, used to send	audiēbās / you were hearing, kept hearing , used to hear
3rd Person, Singular	mittēbat / he, she, it was sending, kept sending, used to send	audiēbat / he, she, it was hearing, kept hearing , used to hear
1st Person, Plural	mittēbāmus / we were sending, kept sending, used to send	audiēbāmus / we were hearing, kept hearing , used to hear
2nd Person, Plural	mittēbātis / you (all) were sending, kept sending, used to send	audiēbātis / you (all) were hearing, kept hearing , used to hear
3rd Person, Plural	mittēbant / they were sending, kept sending, used to send	audiēbant / they were hearing, kept hearing, used to hear

Person & Number	3rd Conjugation *cadō, cadere, cecidī, cāsus:* to fall	4th Conjugation *veniō, venīre, vēnī, ventus:* to come
1st Person, Singular		
2nd Person, Singular		
3rd Person, Singular		
1st Person, Plural		
2nd Person, Plural		
3rd Person, Plural		

Irregular Verbs in the Imperfect Tense / Practice

An irregular verb does not follow a particular, predictable pattern for its conjugations, so we have to spend additional time memorizing these forms. Copy down the forms of the irregular verbs *sum, esse* and *possum, posse,* meaning "to be able to do" in the space below.

Person & Number	Example Irregular Verb / Latin Form *sum, esse:* to be	Example Irregular Verb / Latin Form *possum, posse:* to be able to do
1st Person, Singular	eram / I was	poteram / I was able to do
2nd Person, Singular	eras / you were	poteras / you were able to do
3rd Person, Singular	erat / he, she, it was	poterat / he, she, it was able to do
1st Person, Plural	eramus / we were	poteramus / we were able to do
2nd Person, Plural	eratis / you (all) were	poteratis / you (all) were able to do
3rd Person, Plural	erant / they were	poterant / they were able to do

Person & Number	Example Irregular Verb / Latin Form *sum, esse:* to be	Example Irregular Verb / Latin Form *possum, posse:* to be able to do
1st Person, Singular	______________	______________
2nd Person, Singular	______________	______________
3rd Person, Singular	______________	______________
1st Person, Plural	______________	______________
2nd Person, Plural	______________	______________
3rd Person, Plural	______________	______________

The Imperfect Tense / Practice

Instructions: Please conjugate the following verbs in the imperfect tense, then translate.

Conjugate & Translate: *crociō, crocīre, crocīvī, crocītus*, to croak

Conjugation: ____________________

Singular

1st Singular: ____________________

Translation: ____________________

2nd Singular: ____________________

Translation: ____________________

3rd Singular: ____________________

Translation: ____________________

Plural

1st Plural: ____________________

Translation: ____________________

2nd Plural: ____________________

Translation: ____________________

3rd Plural: ____________________

Translation: ____________________

Conjugate & Translate: *ōrō, ōrāre, ōrāvī, ōrātum*, to pray

Conjugation: ____________________

Singular

1st Singular: ____________________

Translation: ____________________

2nd Singular: ____________________

Translation: ____________________

3rd Singular: ____________________

Translation: ____________________

Plural

1st Plural: ____________________

Translation: ____________________

2nd Plural: ____________________

Translation: ____________________

3rd Plural: ____________________

Translation: ____________________

The Imperfect Tense / Practice

Instructions: Please conjugate the following verbs in the imperfect tense, then translate.

Conjugate & Translate: *dūcō, dūcere, dūxī, ductus*, to carry

Conjugation: ______________________________

Singular

1st Singular: ______________________________

Translation: ______________________________

2nd Singular: ______________________________

Translation: ______________________________

3rd Singular: ______________________________

Translation: ______________________________

Plural

1st Plural: ______________________________

Translation: ______________________________

2nd Plural: ______________________________

Translation: ______________________________

3rd Plural: ______________________________

Translation: ______________________________

Conjugate & Translate: *teneō, tenēre, tenuī, tentus*, to hold

Conjugation: ______________________________

Singular

1st Singular: ______________________________

Translation: ______________________________

2nd Singular: ______________________________

Translation: ______________________________

3rd Singular: ______________________________

Translation: ______________________________

Plural

1st Plural: ______________________________

Translation: ______________________________

2nd Plural: ______________________________

Translation: ______________________________

3rd Plural: ______________________________

Translation: ______________________________

Present Progressive vs. Past Progressive / In English

Instructions: Read over each sentence and identify the tense of the verb written *in blue* as being the present progressive tense or the past progressive tense. Remember that the present progressive action describes an ongoing action that takes place in the present, whereas the past progressive tense describes an action taking place in the past.

Example: I *was going* to the Forum.

Present Progressive (Past Progressive)

1. Romulus *is building* walls on the Palatine Hill.

Present Progressive Past Progressive

2. The sacred geese *are guarding* the Temple to Juno.

Present Progressive Past Progressive

3. Jupiter *was throwing* his thunderbolts.

Present Progressive Past Progressive

4. Remus *was building* his walls on the Aventine Hill.

Present Progressive Past Progressive

5. The Cyclopses *were living* inside of Mount Etna.

Present Progressive Past Progressive

6. The gods *were ruling* from Mount Olympus.

Present Progressive Past Progressive

7. I *am going* to the Forum.

Present Progressive Past Progressive

8. Tarquin *was building* the Cloaca Maxima, a massive sewer system for the Romans.

Present Progressive Past Progressive

9. The Tiber River *is flooding* the streets of Rome.

Present Progressive Past Progressive

10. Romulus *is picking* the first members of the Roman Senate.

Present Progressive Past Progressive

11. Aeneas *was journeying* to Italy when he stopped in Carthage.

Present Progressive Past Progressive

12. The she-wolf *is nursing* the infants Romulus and Remus.

Present Progressive Past Progressive

Present vs. Imperfect Tenses / In English

Instructions: Continue the exercise from the previous page.

12. The she-wolf *is rescuing* the infants Romulus and Remus.

Present Progressive   Past Progressive

13. Hannibal *was riding* an elephant over the Alps.

Present Progressive   Past Progressive

14. Dido *was ruling* the people of Carthage.

Present Progressive   Past Progressive

15.Horatius Cocles *is guarding* the bridge and *is guarding* the city of Rome.

Present Progressive   Past Progressive

16.Gaius Scaevola *was holding* his hand over a fire.

Present Progressive   Past Progressive

17.Lucretia *is knitting* socks for her husband, who is away on campaign.

Present Progressive   Past Progressive

18.Romulus *was seeing* a larger group of birds when he claimed the gods chose his site to be king.

Present Progressive   Past Progressive

x19.Romulus *was building* walls on the Palatine Hill when Remus jumped over them.

Present Progressive   Past Progressive

20.Numa Pompilius, Rome's second king, *is setting up* Rome's religious institutions.

Present Progressive   Past Progressive

21.Tullus Hostilius, Rome's third king, *was fighting* the nearby city of Alba Longa.

Present Progressive   Past Progressive

22.Ancus Marcus, Rome's fourth king, *is defeating* the nearby tribe of the Sabines.

Present Progressive   Past Progressive

23.Tarquin Superbus, Rome seventh and final king, *was building* the Circus Maximus.

Present Progressive   Past Progressive

The Imperfect Tense & Verb Persons

Vocabulary Word / Meaning
legere: to read
studēre: to study
ambulāre / to walk

Instructions: Read over each sentence and identify the person and number for each Latin verb. Write your answers in the space provided under each verb. Note, too, that most of these verbs can stand on their own in a sentence. For these first few exercises, the base is in green, while the ending is italicized and in *blue*. Translate the verb.

Example: *Studebam*: I was studying.

1. studē*bāmus*

Translation: ______________________________

2.studē*bātis*

Translation: ______________________________

3. studē*bat*

Translation: ______________________________

4. studē*bant*

Translation: ______________________________

5. ambulā*bātis*

Translation: ______________________________

6. ambulā*bās*

Translation: ______________________________

7. ambulā*bat*

Translation: ______________________________

8. ambulā*bam*

Translation: ______________________________

9. legē*bam*

Translation: ______________________________

10. legē*bant*

Translation: ______________________________

11. legē*bātis*.

Translation: ______________________________

12. legē*bās*

Translation: ______________________________

13. ambulā*bāmus*

Translation: ______________________________

14. legē*bāmus*

Translation: ______________________________

The Imperfect Tense & Verb Persons

Vocabulary Word / Meaning
discere: to learn
audīre: to hear
portāre: to carry

Instructions: Continue the exercise from the previous page.

14. discē*bās*

Translation: ______________________________

15. portā*bās*

Translation: ______________________________

16. audiē*bās*

Translation: ______________________________

17. discē*bāmus*

Translation: ______________________________

18. audiē*bant*

Translation: ______________________________

19. audiē*bam*

Translation: ______________________________

20. portā*bās*

Translation: ______________________________

21. discē*bam*

Translation: ______________________________

22. discē*bat*

Translation: ______________________________

23. discē*bāmus*

Translation: ______________________________

24. portā*bātis*

Translation: ______________________________

25. portā*bant*

Translation: ______________________________

PRACTICE & REVIEW

The Imperfect Tense & Verb Persons

Vocabulary Word / Meaning
dūcere: to lead
habēre: to have
amāre: to love

Instructions: Continue the exercise from the previous page.

26. audiē***bātis***

Translation: ______________________________

27. audiē***bant***

Translation: ______________________________

28. audiē***bat***

Translation: ______________________________

29. portā***bātis***

Translation: ______________________________

30. discē***bātis***

Translation: ______________________________

30. habē***bant***

Translation: ______________________________

31. dūcē***bam***

Translation: ______________________________

32. habē***bātis***

Translation: ______________________________

33. dūcē***bās***

Translation: ______________________________

34. habe***bam***

Translation: ______________________________

35. dūcē***bat***

Translation: ______________________________

36. habē***bās***

Translation: ______________________________

Practice & Review

The Imperfect Tense & Verb Persons

Vocabulary Word / Meaning
currere: to run
scīre: to know
mutāre: to change

Instructions: Continue the exercise from the previous page.

37. dūcē***bātis***

Translation: ______________________

38. amā***bātis***

Translation: ______________________

39. dūcē***bant***

Translation: ______________________

40. amā***bam***

Translation: ______________________

41. amā***bās***

Translation: ______________________

42. amā***bat***

Translation: ______________________

43. habē***bāmus***

Translation: ______________________

44. amā***bant***

Translation: ______________________

45. habē***bant***

Translation: ______________________

46. mutā***bāmus***

Translation: ______________________

47. currē***bāmus***

Translation: ______________________

The Future Tense

IN ENGLISH, AN action that will take place in the future takes place in the appropriately-named future tense. In Latin likewise, an action that will take place at some point in the future is said to take place in the **future tense**.

In English, we can easily identify the future tense by the helping verb *will* and *shall*. A **helping verb** appears just before a verb to signify the tense and the mood of that particular verb. For example, a sentence like *I am walking to the store* takes place at the present time; *I walked to the store* in past time; whereas the sentence *I will walk to the store* will take place at some point in the future.

In Latin, we form the future tense in two different ways, depending on the conjugation of the verb. The first and second conjugation have one way of forming the future tense, and the third and fourth conjugation have a different way of forming the future tense. Let's learn the way the first and second conjugations form the future tense now.

Recall that a verb falls into one of four different conjugations, each of which is marked by a significant vowel found in its second principal part. The first conjugation has a long *ā* as its significant vowel, *ā* as in the verbs ***amāre***, ***parāre***, or ***portāre***. The second conjugation has a long *ē* as its significant vowel, *ē* as in the verbs ***habēre***, ***movēre***, or ***monēre***.

In the first and second conjugation, the future tense is formed by adding two letters in between the stem of that verb and its personal endings. These letters are -*bo* and -*bi*, *bo* in the first person singular and -*bi* for the rest of its endings.

These future tense markers are similar to those of the imperfect tense (the letters -*ba*). Providing you remember to use the helping verb *will* to translate any word you see with the letters -*bi* between the stem of a verb and its personal endings, the future tense should give you no trouble.

BIG IDEA

The future tense refers to an action that will take place in the future. The first and second conjugation form the future tense by adding the letters -bi *in between the stem of the verb and its personal endings, whereas the third and fourth conjugations have endings that look like a second conjugation, present tense verb—so watch out, and make note of a verb's conjugation!*

New Vocabulary

Future Tense
An action that will take place at some point in the future.

Helping Verb
In English, this is a word placed next to a verb to signify the tense or the mood of the verb. Examples include *will*, *would*, *should*, among others.

Review Vocabulary

Tense
The time an action takes and what kind of an action it is.

Tense Markers
Letters between the *base* of a verb and its personal endings indicating the tense of that verb.

Imperfect Tense
The imperfect tense refers to an ongoing, habitual action in the past.

Here's an example of the future tense and how it is formed in the first and second conjugation.

Here's another example, albeit slightly more difficult: *parābō*:

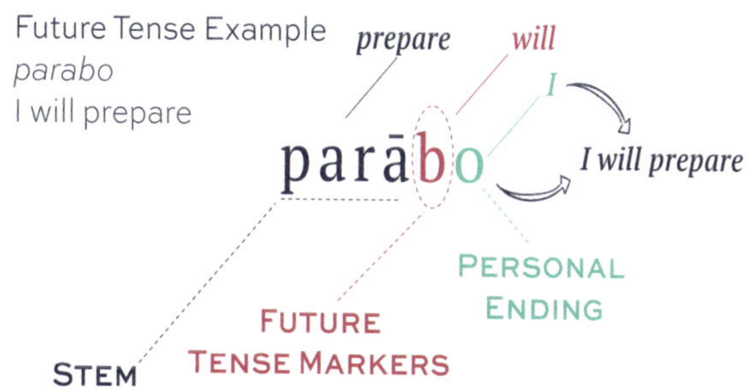

The first person singular form drops the - *i* from the future tense marker, to avoid a linguistic phenomenon called "collision" and thus prevent two vowels from being placed next to each other. Aside from this occurrence, the endings in the future tense for the first and second conjugation are straight forward, as in the chart below:

	1st Conjugation *parō, parāre: to prepare*	2nd Conjugation *moveō, movēre: to move*
1st Person / Singular	parābō / I will prepare	movēbō / I will move
2nd Person / Singular	parābis / you will prepare	movēbis / you will move
3rd Person / Singular	parābit / he, she, it will prepare	movēbit / he, she, it will move
1st Person / Plural	parābimus / we will prepare	movēbimus / we will move
2nd Person / Plural	parābitis / you (all) will prepare	movēbitis/ you (all) will move
3rd Person / Plural	parābunt / they will prepare	movēbunt / they will move

The third and fourth conjugations do not form the future tense in this straightforward, predictable way. Recall that third conjugation verbs have a short - *e* as their significant vowel as in the verbs *mittō, mittere* and *iaciō, iacere*.

This - *e* changes to an - *i* in its chart. In the present tense, the third and fourth conjugation have the letter - *i* in between the verb stem and the personal endings. In their charts, they conjugate like this:

3rd Conjugation Present Tense *mittō, mittere: to send*	**4th Conjugation Present Tense** *audiō, audīre: to hear, listen*
mittō / I send	audiō / I hear
mittis / you send	audīs / you hear
mittit / he, she send	audit / he, she hears
mittimus we send	audīmus we hear
mittitis / you (all) send	audītis / you (all) hear
mittunt / they send	audiunt / they hear

The third and fourth conjugation have the same endings for future tense verbs. But instead of future tense markers, they have endings that look like the present forms of second conjugation verbs—which can get very confusing, very quickly! Here are the charts for the third and fourth conjugations in the future tense.

3rd Conjugation Future Tense *mittō, mittere: to send*	**4th Conjugation Future Tense** *audiō, audīre: to hear, listen*
mittam / I will send	audiam / I will hear
mittēs / you will send	audiēs / you will hear
mittet / he, she will send	audiet / he, she will hear
mittēmus we send	audiēmus we will hear
mittētis / you (all) will send	audiētis / you (all) will hear
mittent / they will send	audient / they will hear

The key to identifying the future tense is to know whether or not a verb is in the third or fourth conjugation. The importance of distinguishing a third conjugation verb from a second conjugation verb cannot be underestimated. In memorizing vocabulary, be sure to write at least the first and the second principal parts of that verb, paying careful attention to its significant vowel. If the vowel is an - *e*, note whether or not that - *e* has a macron over it—that - *ē* is the significant vowel for the second conjugation—or if it lacks a macron and is a short - *e*. Long -*ē* is second, and -*e* short is third.

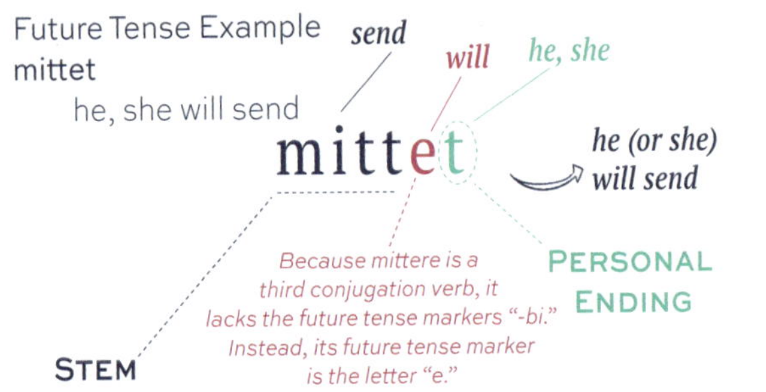

If it has an - *ī* as its significant vowel, that verb is in the fourth conjugation and conjugates in the same way.

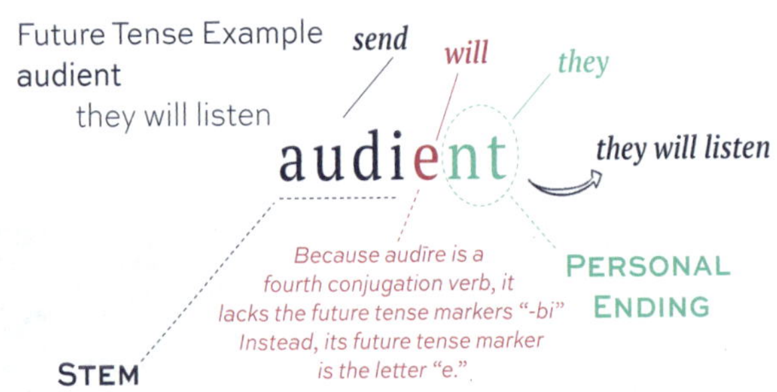

Once you recognize the verb as being in the third or fourth conjugation, remember that its future tense forms are similar to its present tense forms. Copy down the charts for the third and fourth conjugation until you memorize them and feel more comfortable recognizing them. While the future tense is difficult at first, you can memorize this new chart and commit it to mastery with just a little bit of practice. *Bona fortuna*!

Lesson Review Questions

1. What is the future tense? How do we translate it?

2. How do we form the future tense in the first and second conjugations?

3. How do we form the future tense in the third and fourth conjugations?

4. Why is it important to memorize the conjugation of a verb?

The Future Tense / Practice

Instructions: Please conjugate the following verbs in the space below. Remember that first and second conjugation verbs use the future tense markers - *bo* and *-bi.*

Future Tense / *The verb refers to an action that will happen in the* **future**.

Person & Number	1st Conjugation *amō, amāre: to love*	2nd Conjugation *habeō, habēre: to have*
1st Person, Singular	amābō / I will love	habēbō / I will have
2nd Person, Singular	amābis / you will love	habēbis / you will have
3rd Person, Singular	amābit / he, she, it will love	habēbit / he, she, it will have
1st Person, Plural	amābimus we will love	habēbimus / we will have
2nd Person, Plural	amābitis / you (all) will love	habēbitis / you (all) will have
3rd Person, Plural	amābunt / they will love	habēbunt / they will have

Person & Number	1st Conjugation *laudō, laudāre, laudāvī, laudātus:* to praise	2nd Conjugation *doceō, docēre, docuī, doctus:* to teach
1st Person, Singular		
2nd Person, Singular		
3rd Person, Singular		
1st Person, Plural		
2nd Person, Plural		
3rd Person, Plural		

The Future Tense / Practice

Instructions: Please conjugate the following verbs in the space below. Remember that third and fourth conjugation verbs do not use the future tense markers - *bo* and *-bi.*

Future Tense / *The verb refers to an action that will happen in the* **future**.

Person & Number	3rd Conjugation *mittō, mittere: to send*	4th Conjugation *audiō, audīre: to hear*
1st Person, Singular	mittam / I will send	audiam / I will hear
2nd Person, Singular	mittēs / you will send	audiēs / you will hear
3rd Person, Singular	mittet / he, she, it will send	audiet / he, she, it will hear
1st Person, Plural	mittēmus / we will send	audiēmus / we will hear
2nd Person, Plural	mittētis / you (all) will send	audiētis / you (all) will hear
3rd Person, Plural	mittent / they will send	audient / they will hear

Person & Number	3rd Conjugation *tangō, tangere, tetigī, tāctus: to touch*	4th Conjugation *sciō, scīre, scīvī, scītus: to know*
1st Person, Singular		
2nd Person, Singular		
3rd Person, Singular		
1st Person, Plural		
2nd Person, Plural		
3rd Person, Plural		

Irregular Verbs in the Future Tense / Practice

An irregular verb does not follow a particular, predictable pattern for its conjugations, so we have to spend additional time memorizing these forms. Copy down the forms of the irregular verbs in the space below.

Person & Number	Example Irregular Verb / Latin Form *sum, esse, fuī, futurus:* to be	Example Irregular Verb / Latin Form *possum, posse, potuī, futurus:* to be
1st Person, Singular	erō / I will be	poterō / I will be able to
2nd Person, Singular	eris / you will be	poteris / you will be able to
3rd Person, Singular	erit / he, she, it will be	poterit / he, she, it will be able to
1st Person, Plural	erimus / we will be	poterimus / we will be able to
2nd Person, Plural	eritis / you (all) will be	poteritis / you (all) will be able to
3rd Person, Plural	erunt / they will be	poterunt / they will be able to

Person & Number	Example Irregular Verb *sum, esse, fuī, futurus:* to be	Example Irregular Verb *possum, posse, potuī, futurus:* to be
1st Person, Singular		
2nd Person, Singular		
3rd Person, Singular		
1st Person, Plural		
2nd Person, Plural		
3rd Person, Plural		

The Future Tense / Practice

Instructions: Please identify the correct conjugation of each verb, then write out the various forms for the future tense of the following verbs.

Conjugate & Translate: portō, portāre, *to carry*

Conjugation: ______________________________

Singular

1st Singular: ______________________________

Translation: ______________________________

2nd Singular: ______________________________

Translation: ______________________________

3rd Singular: ______________________________

Translation: ______________________________

Plural

1st Plural: ______________________________

Translation: ______________________________

2nd Plural: ______________________________

Translation: ______________________________

3rd Plural: ______________________________

Translation: ______________________________

Conjugate & Translate: iaciō, iacere, *to throw*

Conjugation: ______________________________

Singular

1st Singular: ______________________________

Translation: ______________________________

2nd Singular: ______________________________

Translation: ______________________________

3rd Singular: ______________________________

Translation: ______________________________

Plural

1st Plural: ______________________________

Translation: ______________________________

2nd Plural: ______________________________

Translation: ______________________________

3rd Plural: ______________________________

Translation: ______________________________

The Future Tense / Practice

Instructions: Please identify the correct conjugation of each verb, then write out the various forms for the future tense of the following verbs.

Conjugate & Translate: *saepiō, saepīre, saepsi, saeptus*, to hedge in

Conjugation: ________________________________

Singular

1st Singular: ________________________________

Translation: ________________________________

2nd Singular: ________________________________

Translation: ________________________________

3rd Singular: ________________________________

Translation: ________________________________

Plural

1st Plural: ________________________________

Translation: ________________________________

2nd Plural: ________________________________

Translation: ________________________________

3rd Plural: ________________________________

Translation: ________________________________

Conjugate & Translate: *negō, negāre, negāvī, negātus*, to deny

Conjugation: ________________________________

Singular

1st Singular: ________________________________

Translation: ________________________________

2nd Singular: ________________________________

Translation: ________________________________

3rd Singular: ________________________________

Translation: ________________________________

Plural

1st Plural: ________________________________

Translation: ________________________________

2nd Plural: ________________________________

Translation: ________________________________

3rd Plural: ________________________________

Translation: ________________________________

The Future Tense / Practice

Instructions: Please identify the correct conjugation of each verb, then write out the various forms for the future tense of the following verbs.

Conjugate & Translate: *mūgiō, mūgīre, mūgīvī, mūgītus*, to bellow

Conjugation: ______________________________

Singular

1st Singular: ______________________________

Translation: ______________________________

2nd Singular: ______________________________

Translation: ______________________________

3rd Singular: ______________________________

Translation: ______________________________

Plural

1st Plural: ______________________________

Translation: ______________________________

2nd Plural: ______________________________

Translation: ______________________________

3rd Plural: ______________________________

Translation: ______________________________

Conjugate & Translate: *videō, vidēre, vīdī, vīsum*, to see

Conjugation: ______________________________

Singular

1st Singular: ______________________________

Translation: ______________________________

2nd Singular: ______________________________

Translation: ______________________________

3rd Singular: ______________________________

Translation: ______________________________

Plural

1st Plural: ______________________________

Translation: ______________________________

2nd Plural: ______________________________

Translation: ______________________________

3rd Plural: ______________________________

Translation: ______________________________

PRACTICE & REVIEW

Present Progressive vs. Past Progressive vs. Future / In English

Instructions: Read over each sentence and identify the tense of the verb written *in blue* as being the present progressive tense or the past progressive tense. Remember that the present progressive action describes an ongoing action that takes place in the present, whereas the past progressive tense describes an action taking place in the past.

Example: I *will go* to the Forum.

Present Progressive Past Progressive (Future)

1. Romulus *will found* the city of Rome.

Simple Progressive Past Progressive Future

2. The sacred geese *will save* Rome from the Gauls.

Simple Progressive Past Progressive Future

3. Jupiter *is throwing* his thunderbolts from the sky.

Simple Progressive Past Progressive Future

4. Remus *was building* his walls on the Aventine Hill.

Simple Progressive Past Progressive Future

5. The Cyclopses *are living* inside of Mount Etna.

Simple Progressive Past Progressive Future

6. The Cyclopses *were making* Jupiter's thunderbolts.

Simple Progressive Past Progressive Future

7. Mount Vesuvius *will erupt* in AD 79.

Simple Progressive Past Progressive Future

8. Tarquin *is building* the Cloaca Maxima, a massive sewer system for the Romans.

Simple Progressive Past Progressive Future

9. The Tiber River *will flood* the streets of Rome.

Simple Progressive Past Progressive Future

10. Romulus is planning the abduction of the Sabines.

Simple Progressive Past Progressive Future

11. Aeneas *was journeying* to Italy when he stopped in Carthage.

Simple Progressive Past Progressive Future

12. The she-wolf *is nursing* the infants Romulus and Remus.

Simple Progressive Past Progressive Future

Present Progressive vs. Past Progressive vs. Future / In English

Instructions: Continue the exercise from the previous page.

12. A she-wolf *will rescue* Romulus and Remus.

Simple Progressive   Past Progressive   Future

13. The evil Amulius *is planning* to murder the infants Romulus and Remus

Simple Progressive   Past Progressive   Future

14. Dido *was ruling* the people of Carthage.

Simple Progressive   Past Progressive   Future

15. Horatius Cocles *was guarding* the bridge when the king of Clusium attacked Rome.

Simple Progressive   Past Progressive   Future

16. Aeneas *will stop* at Carthage.

Simple Progressive   Past Progressive   Future

17. Lucretia *was knitting* socks for her husband, who was away on campaign.

Simple Progressive   Past Progressive   Future

18. Romulus *will see* a larger group of birds which he interprets as the gods' favor on his settlement.

Simple Progressive   Past Progressive   Future

19. Remus *will see* the first group of birds which he interprets as the gods' favor on his settlement.

Simple Progressive   Past Progressive   Future

20. Numa Pompilius, Rome's second king, *will establish* Rome's religious institutions.

Simple Progressive   Past Progressive   Future

21. Tullus Hostilius, Rome's third king, *is fighting* the nearby city of Alba Longa.

Simple Progressive   Past Progressive   Future

22. Ancus Marcus, Rome's fourth king, *will defeat* the nearby tribe of the Sabines.

Simple Progressive   Past Progressive   Future

23. Tarquin Superbus, Rome seventh and final king, *is building* the Circus Maximus.

Simple Progressive   Past Progressive   Future

24. The Romans Brutus and Collatinus *will found* the Roman Republic.

Simple Progressive   Past Progressive   Future

The Future Tense & Verb Persons

Vocabulary Word / Meaning
legere: to read
studēre: to study
ambulāre / to walk

Instructions: Read over each example and identify the person and number for each Latin verb. Write your answers in the space provided under each verb. Note, too, that most of these verbs can stand on their own in a sentence. For these first few exercises, the base is in green, while the ending is italicized and in ***blue***. Translate the verb.

Example: ***Studebō***: I was studying.

1. stud*ē**bimus***

Person & Number: ______________________________

Translation: ______________________________

2. stud*ē**bitis***

Person & Number: ______________________________

Translation: ______________________________

3. stud*ē**bit***

Person & Number: ______________________________

Translation: ______________________________

4. stud*ē**bunt***

Person & Number: ______________________________

Translation: ______________________________

5. ambulā***bitis***

Person & Number: ______________________________

Translation: ______________________________

6. ambulā***bis***

Person & Number: ______________________________

Translation: ______________________________

7. ambulā***bit***

Person & Number: ______________________________

Translation: ______________________________

8. ambulā***bimus***

Person & Number: ______________________________

Translation: ______________________________

9. leg***am***

Person & Number: ______________________________

Translation: ______________________________

The Future Tense & Verb Persons

Vocabulary Word / Meaning
discere: to learn
audīre: to hear
portāre: to carry

Instructions: Continue the exercise from the previous page.

10. leg*ent*

Person & Number: ______________________

Translation: ______________________

11. leg*ēs*.

Person & Number: ______________________

Translation: ______________________

12. leg*ētis*

Person & Number: ______________________

Translation: ______________________

13. ambulā*bimus*

Person & Number: ______________________

Translation: ______________________

14. leg*ēmus*

Person & Number: ______________________

Translation: ______________________

14. disc*ēs*

Person & Number: ______________________

Translation: ______________________

15. portā*bis*

Person & Number: ______________________

Translation: ______________________

16. audi*ēs*

Person & Number: ______________________

Translation: ______________________

7. disc*ēmus*

Person & Number: ______________________

Translation: ______________________

18. audi*ent*

Person & Number: ______________________

Translation: ______________________

Practice & Review

The Future Tense & Verb Persons

Instructions: Continue the exercise from the previous page.

Vocabulary Word / Meaning
dūcere: to lead
habēre: to have
amāre: to love

19. audi*am*

Person & Number: ______________________

Translation: ______________________

20. portā*bis*

Person & Number: ______________________

Translation: ______________________

21. disc*am*

Person & Number: ______________________

Translation: ______________________

22. disc*et*

Person & Number: ______________________

Translation: ______________________

23. disc*ēmus*

Person & Number: ______________________

Translation: ______________________

24. portā*bitis*

Person & Number: ______________________

Translation: ______________________

25. portā*bunt*

Person & Number: ______________________

Translation: ______________________

26. audi*ētis*

Person & Number: ______________________

Translation: ______________________

27. audi*ent*

Person & Number: ______________________

Translation: ______________________

28. audi*ent*

Person & Number: ______________________

Translation: ______________________

Practice & Review

The Future Tense & Verb Persons

Instructions: Continue the exercise from the previous page.

29. portā***bitis***

Person & Number: ______________________

Translation: ______________________

30. disc***ētis***

Person & Number: ______________________

Translation: ______________________

31. dūc***am***

Person & Number: ______________________

Translation: ______________________

32. habē***bitis***

Person & Number: ______________________

Translation: ______________________

33. dūc***ēs***

Person & Number: ______________________

Translation: ______________________

34. habē***bunt***

Person & Number: ______________________

Translation: ______________________

35. dūc***et***

Person & Number: ______________________

Translation: ______________________

36. habē***bō***

Person & Number: ______________________

Translation: ______________________

37. dūc***ētis***

Person & Number: ______________________

Translation: ______________________

38. amā***bitis***

Person & Number: ______________________

Translation: ______________________

The Present, Imperfect, & Future Tense

Instructions: Read over each example and identify what tense, person, and number is for each Latin verb. Write your answers in the space provided under each verb.

Example: *Studebō*: Future Tense, First Person, Singular.

1. ambula**t**

Tense: ______________________________

Person & Number : ____________________

2. studē**bātis**

Tense: ______________________________

Person & Number : ____________________

3. ambulā**bat**

Tense: ______________________________

Person & Number : ____________________

4. ambulā**bāmus**

Tense: ______________________________

Person & Number : ____________________

5. ambulā**bitis**

Tense: ______________________________

Person & Number : ____________________

6. ambulā**mus**

Tense: ______________________________

Person & Number : ____________________

7. ambulā**bit**

Tense: ______________________________

Person & Number : ____________________

8. ambulā**bātis**

Tense: ______________________________

Person & Number : ____________________

9. leg**am**

Tense: ______________________________

Person & Number : ____________________

10. leg***unt***

Tense: ______________________________

Person & Number : ____________________

The Present, Imperfect, & Future Tense

Instructions: Continue the exercise from the previous page.

11. studē***bitis***

Tense: ______________________________

Person & Number : ______________________

12. leg*is*

Tense: ______________________________

Person & Number : ______________________

13. ambulā**bimus**

Tense: ______________________________

Person & Number : ______________________

14. studeō

Tense: ______________________________

Person & Number : ______________________

14. ambulā**tis**

Translation: ______________________

15. studē**bam**

Tense: ______________________________

Person & Number : ______________________

16. studē**bātis**

Tense: ______________________________

Person & Number : ______________________

17. studē**bimus**

Tense: ______________________________

Person & Number : ______________________

18. leg**it**

Tense: ______________________________

Person & Number : ______________________

19. leg**et**

Tense: ______________________________

Person & Number : ______________________

The Perfect Tense

IN ENGLISH, we think of actions as ongoing, habitual, or completed. We call these items the aspect of a verb. That is, an action keeps happening over an indefinite period of time, or the action has already happened and is, in a sense, finished or completed. In English, we label this kind of action as the **simple past tense**.

For the Romans, they considered a completed, finished action to be perfect, perfect in the sense that the action did not need anything else and was in that sense, complete. If we think of a "perfect" weekend or a "perfect" novel, we are thinking of a weekend or novel that lacks nothing and needs no additions or changes.

In Latin, an action that took place in the past is, in this sense, *completed* or *perfect* since it cannot be changed. And hence we have the **perfect tense**, a tense that signifies a completed action that took place in the past. The Latin perfect tense corresponds to the English simple past tense.

In reading Latin, we translate actions in the perfect tense by adding the letters -*ed* onto the end of regular verbs. The sentence *I am walking* is in the present tense, whereas the sentence *I walked* is in the simple past tense, with the letters -*ed* signifying that the action took place in the past and was completed. English also has a number of irregular verbs that change their spelling if the action happened in the present or in the past, as in the examples *catch* (present tense) vs. *caught* (past tense), *go* (present) vs. *went* (past), and other similar examples.

Latin verbs change into an entirely different form to signify the perfect tense. The perfect tense is formed from the perfect tense stem, derived from the third principal part. Here are some examples:

- *amō, amāre,* **amāvī**, *amatus:* to love
- *habeō, habēre,* **habuī**, *habitus:* to have
- *mittō, mittere,* **mīsī**, *missus:* to send
- *audiō, audīre,* **audīvī**, *audītus:* to hear

To form the perfect tense, we have to first identify the third principal part. In the examples above, the third principal part is literally the word that comes third in that list and includes *amāvī*, *habuī*, *mīsī*, and *audīvī*. From there, we add on the appropriate personal endings as needed. If we want to say, "I loved," we use the form *amāvī*; If we want to say, "We had," we use the form *habuimus*; "you all sent," the form *mīsistis*; "they heard" or "they listened," *audiērunt*. The different parts of a perfect tense verb look like this:

We should note that the perfect tense may have different personal endings, but the corresponding verb persons do not change. A first person singular verb still uses the pronoun *I* in the perfect tense as it does in the present tense, whereas a third person plural verb

Review Vocabulary

Verb
A word that refers to an action or a state of being.

Tense
The time an action takes and what kind of an action it is.

New Vocabulary

Past Perfect Tense
In English, this tense refers to a completed action that took place in the past.

Perfect Tense
The perfect tense refers to a completed action that took place in the past.

Perfect Tense Markers
The perfect tense markers include the letters *- s*, *- v*, and *- u* and are found between the perfect tense stem and the personal endings.

uses the pronoun *they* in the perfect tense as it does in the present or imperfect. With the perfect tense, we are adding a new set of endings to our Latin toolbox.

The third principal part is always the first person singular, perfect tense form of a verb. One cannot necessarily guess what a perfect tense verb will look like, so it is best to memorize all four principal parts as you learn new vocabulary. To help us identify the perfect tense, the letters *-v*, *-s,* and sometimes *- u* serve as **perfect tense markers**. They appear on the perfect tense stem just before the personal endings, as in the verb forms *amāvī, habuī,* and *mīsī*, among other perfect tense forms. The endings for the perfect tense are as follows:

Person & Number	*Endings*	*Sample Verb* amō, amāre, amavī, amatus
1st Person Singular	- ī . . .	amāvī / I loved
2nd Person Singular	- istī / you . . .	amāvistī / you loved
3rd Person Singular	- it / he, she, it . . .	amāvit / he, she, it loved
1st Person Plural	- imus / he, she, it . . .	amāvimus / he, she, it loved
2nd Person Plural	- istis / you (all) . . .	amāvistis / you (all) loved
3rd Person Plural	- ērunt / they . . .	amāvērunt / they loved

To summarize, the perfect tense is used for completed actions that took place in the past. In reading Latin, we translate a perfect tense verb by adding the letters *-ed* onto the end of a regular verb (as in *I walked*) or by using the appropriate irregular verb form (as in *I ran*). If we need to, we can also use the auxiliary helping verb *have* for the perfect tense, signaling that the action is taking place in the past.

In Latin, the perfect tense is formed from the perfect tense stem. The perfect tense stem is the third principal part of a verb, and if we memorize the four principal parts, we should be able to recognize perfect tense verbs with relative ease. Still, the perfect tense does have its own perfect tense markers that help us identify the perfect tense. These markers include the letters *-v, -s,* and *-u,* which appear after the perfect tense stem and its personal endings. In reading Latin, we translate a verb in the perfect tense in the simple past tense.

Perfect Tense Forms

	Example 1st Conjugation Verb *parō, parāre, parāvī, parātus:* to prepare	Example 2nd Conjugation Verb *moveō, movēre, mōvī, mōtus:* to move
1st Person Singular	parāvī / I prepared	mōvī / I moved
2nd Person Singular	parāvistī/ you prepared	mōvistī / you moved
3rd Person Singular	parāvit/ he, she, it prepared	mōvit / he, she, it moved
1st Person Plural	parāvimus / we prepared	mōvimus / we moved
2nd Person Plural	parāvistis / you (all) prepared	mōvistis / you (all) moved
3rd Person Plural	parāvērunt / they prepared	mōvērunt / they moved

BIG IDEA

The perfect tense refers to a completed action that happened in the past. The perfect tense is formed from the third principal part and has the endings - ī, - istī, - it, - imus, - istis, *and* - ērunt. *The perfect tense is translated into English like the simple past tense, often by adding the letters* - ed *onto the end of a regular verb.*

Perfect Tense Forms

	Example 3rd Conjugation Verb *mittō, mittere, mīsī, missus:* to send	Example 4th Conjugation Verb *audiō, audīre, audīvī, audītus:* to hear
1st Person Singular	mīsī / I sent	audīvī / I heard
2nd Person Singular	mīsistī / you sent	audīvistī / you heard
3rd Person Singular	mīsit / he, she, it sent	audīvit / he, she, it heard
1st Person Plural	mīsimus / we sent	audīvimus / we heard
2nd Person Plural	mīsistis / you (all) sent	audīvistis/ you (all) heard
3rd Person Plural	mīsērunt / they sent	audīvērunt / they heard

	Example Irregular Verb *sum, esse, fuī, futūrus:* to be	Example Irregular Verb *eō, īre, ivī or iī, itus:* to go
1st Person Singular	fuī / I was, I have been	īvī or iī / I went
2nd Person Singular	fuistī / you were, you have been	īvistī or īstī / you went
3rd Person Singular	fuit / he, she, it was, has been	īvit or iit / he, she, it went
1st Person Plural	fuimus / we were, we have been	iimus / we went
2nd Person Plural	fuistis / you (all) were, you (all) have been	īvistis *or* īstis / you (all) went
3rd Person Plural	fuērunt / they were, they have been	iērunt / they went

Lesson Review Questions

1. How is a perfect tense action "complete" or "perfect"?

2. Where do we find the perfect tense stem?

3. What is a "tense marker"? What are the perfect tense markers?

4. How do we translate a verb in the perfect tense?

The Perfect Tense / Practice

Instructions: Write the Latin Form in the first column and the English translation in the second column for each verbs listed below in the perfect tense.

Person & Number	1st Conjugation / Latin Form *portō, portāre, portavī, portatus*: to carry	English Translation
1st Person, Singular / I __		
2nd Person, Singular / you __		
3rd Person, Singular / he, she, it __		
1st Person, Plural / we __		
2nd Person, Plural / you (impl. pl.) __		
3rd Person, Plural / they __		

Person & Number	2nd Conjugation / Latin Form moveō, movēre, movī, motus *to move*	English Translation
1st Person, Singular / I __		
2nd Person, Singular / you __		
3rd Person, Singular / he, she, it __		
1st Person, Plural / we __		
2nd Person, Plural / you (impl. pl.) __		
3rd Person, Plural / they __		

The Perfect Tense / Practice

Instructions: Write the Latin Form in the first column and the English translation in the second column for each verb listed below in the perfect tense.

Person & Number	Example 4th Conjugation Verb *adveniō, advenīre, advēni, adventūrus* to come upon	Example Irregular Verb / Latin Form *possum, posse, potuī*: to be able to do
1st Person, Singular / I __		
2nd Person, Singular / you __		
3rd Person, Singular / he, she, it __		
1st Person, Plural / we __		
2nd Person, Plural / you (impl. pl.) __		
3rd Person, Plural / they__		

Person & Number	Example Irregular Verb *sum, esse, fuī, futurus*: to be	Example 4th Conjugation *audiō, audīre, audīvī, audītus*: to hear
1st Person, Singular / I __		
2nd Person, Singular / you __		
3rd Person, Singular / he, she, it __		
1st Person, Plural / we __		
2nd Person, Plural / you (impl. pl.) __		
3rd Person, Plural / they __		

The Past Tense & Irregular Verbs (in English)

Instructions: Read over each example and identify whether the verb is *regular* or *irregular* by circling the appropriate choice. Then note the person, tense, and the number of that English verb.

Example: We went to the store.

Person / Number: 1st person, plural

Tense: Past Tense

Regular or *Irregular* (circled)

1. Romulus went to the Forum.

Person / Number:____________________________

Tense: __________________________________

Regular or *Irregular*

2. The soldiers carried shields and spears.

Person / Number:____________________________

Tense: __________________________________

Regular or *Irregular*

3. Aeneas journeyed to Rome by sea.

Person / Number:____________________________

Tense: __________________________________

Regular or *Irregular*

4. Appius Claudius built the Via Appia.

Person / Number:____________________________

Tense: __________________________________

Regular or *Irregular*

5. Hannibal invaded Italy by way of the Alps.

Person / Number:____________________________

Tense: __________________________________

Regular or *Irregular*

The Past Tense & Irregular Verbs (in English)

Instructions: Continue the exercise from the previous page.

6. The Tiber River flows through Rome.

Person / Number:______________________________

Tense: ______________________________

Regular or *Irregular*

7. Rome has seven hills.

Person / Number:______________________________

Tense: ______________________________

Regular or *Irregular*

8. Brutus assassinated Julius Caesar.

Person / Number:______________________________

Tense: ______________________________

Regular or *Irregular*

8. Tarquin Superbus ruled as Rome's last king.

Person / Number:______________________________

Tense: ______________________________

Regular or *Irregular*

9. The Roman monarchy had seven kings.

Person / Number:______________________________

Tense: ______________________________

Regular or *Irregular*

10. The she-wolf nurses Romulus and Remus.

Person / Number:______________________________

Tense: ______________________________

Regular or *Irregular*

The Past Tense & Irregular Verbs (in English)

Instructions: Continue the exercise from the previous page.

11. Romulus fought with his brother, Remus.

Person / Number:______________________________

Tense: _______________________________________

Regular or *Irregular*

12. Remus saw the first omen.

Person / Number:______________________________

Tense: _______________________________________

Regular or *Irregular*

13. The shepherd rescues Romulus and Remus .

Person / Number:______________________________

Tense: _______________________________________

Regular or *Irregular*

14. Appius Claudius built the Via Appia.

Person / Number:______________________________

Tense: _______________________________________

Regular or *Irregular*

15. Cicero lives on the Palatine Hill.

Person / Number:______________________________

Tense: _______________________________________

Regular or *Irregular*

16. Caesar grew up in the Suburra.

Person / Number:______________________________

Tense: _______________________________________

Regular or *Irregular*

The Perfect Tense / Practice

Instructions: Please conjugate the following verbs in the perfect tense.

Conjugate & Translate: *scrībō, scrībere, scrīpsī, scrīptus*, to write

Conjugation: ______________________________

Singular

1st Singular: ______________________________

Translation: ______________________________

2nd Singular: ______________________________

Translation: ______________________________

3rd Singular: ______________________________

Translation: ______________________________

Plural

1st Plural: ______________________________

Translation: ______________________________

2nd Plural: ______________________________

Translation: ______________________________

3rd Plural: ______________________________

Translation: ______________________________

Conjugate & Translate: *sentiō, sentīre, sēnsī, sēnsus*, to feel

Conjugation: ______________________________

Singular

1st Singular: ______________________________

Translation: ______________________________

2nd Singular: ______________________________

Translation: ______________________________

3rd Singular: ______________________________

Translation: ______________________________

Plural

1st Plural: ______________________________

Translation: ______________________________

2nd Plural: ______________________________

Translation: ______________________________

3rd Plural: ______________________________

Translation: ______________________________

The Perfect Tense / Practice

Instructions: Continue the exercise from the previous page.

Conjugate & Translate: *putō, putāre, putāvī, putātus*, to think

Conjugation: ______________________

Singular

1st Singular: ______________________

Translation: ______________________

2nd Singular: ______________________

Translation: ______________________

3rd Singular: ______________________

Translation: ______________________

Plural

1st Plural: ______________________

Translation: ______________________

2nd Plural: ______________________

Translation: ______________________

3rd Plural: ______________________

Translation: ______________________

Conjugate & Translate: *valeō, valēre, valuī, valitūrus*: to be well

Conjugation: ______________________

Singular

1st Singular: ______________________

Translation: ______________________

2nd Singular: ______________________

Translation: ______________________

3rd Singular: ______________________

Translation: ______________________

Plural

1st Plural: ______________________

Translation: ______________________

2nd Plural: ______________________

Translation: ______________________

3rd Plural: ______________________

Translation: ______________________

PRACTICE & REVIEW

The Perfect Tense & Verb Persons

Instructions: Read over each sentence and identify the person and number for each Latin verb. Write your answers in the space provided under each verb. Note, too, that most of these verbs can stand on their own in a sentence. For these first few exercises, the base is in green, while the ending is italicized and in *blue*. Translate the verb.

Verb #1: *ambulō, ambulāre, ambulāvī, ambulatus: to walk*

1. ambulāv**istī**

Person / Number: ______________________________

Translation: ______________________________

2. ambulāv**it**

Person / Number: ______________________________

Translation: ______________________________

3. ambulāv**ērunt**

Person / Number: ______________________________

Translation: ______________________________

4. ambulāv**istis**

Translation: ______________________________

5. ambulāv**ī**

Person / Number: ______________________________

Translation: ______________________________

Verb #2: *habeō, habēre, habuī, habitus:* to have

6. habu**istis**

Person / Number: ______________________________

Translation: ______________________________

7. habu**istī**

Person / Number: ______________________________

Translation: ______________________________

8. habu**ī**

Person / Number: ______________________________

Translation: ______________________________

The Perfect Tense & Verb Persons

Instructions: Continue the exercise from the previous page.

9. habuērunt

Person / Number: ______________________________

Translation: ______________________________

10.habuimus

Person / Number: ______________________________

Translation: ______________________________

Verb #3: *veniō, venīre, vēnī, ventus:* to come

11. vēnī

Person / Number: ______________________________

Translation: ______________________________

12. vēnistī

Person / Number: ______________________________

Translation: ______________________________

13. vēnimus

Person / Number: ______________________________

Translation: ______________________________

14. vēnērunt

Person / Number: ______________________________

Translation: ______________________________

15. vēnistis

Person / Number: ______________________________

Translation: ______________________________

16. vēnit

Person / Number: ______________________________

Translation: ______________________________

Verb #4: *portō, portāre, portāvī, portātus:* to carry

17. portāvī

Person / Number: ______________________________

Translation: ______________________________

The Perfect Tense & Verb Persons

Instructions: Continue the exercise from the previous page.

18. portāvērunt

Person / Number: ______________________

Translation: ______________________

19. portāvistis

Person / Number: ______________________

Translation: ______________________

20. portāvimus

Person / Number: ______________________

Translation: ______________________

21. portāvit

Person / Number: ______________________

Translation: ______________________

22. portāvistī

Person / Number: ______________________

Translation: ______________________

Verb #5: *missō, mittere, misī, missus:* to send

23. mīsī

Person / Number: ______________________

Translation: ______________________

24. mīsērunt

Person / Number: ______________________

Translation: ______________________

25. mīsīt

Person / Number: ______________________

Translation: ______________________

26. mīsistī

Person / Number: ______________________

Translation: ______________________

27. mīsimus

Person / Number: ______________________

Translation: ______________________

The Perfect Tense & Verb Persons

Instructions: Continue the exercise from the previous page.

Verb #6: *amō, amāre, amāvī, amatus:* to throw

23. amāvī

Person / Number: ______________________

Translation: ______________________

24. amāvīstī

Person / Number: ______________________

Translation: ______________________

25. amāvērunt

Person / Number: ______________________

Translation: ______________________

26. amāvīmus

Person / Number: ______________________

Translation: ______________________

27. amāvīstis

Person / Number: ______________________

Translation: ______________________

28. amāvīt

Person / Number: ______________________

Translation: ______________________

Verb #7: *eō, īrē, iī or ivī, itus:* to go

23. ivī

Person / Number: ______________________

Translation: ______________________

24. ivimus

Person / Number: ______________________

Translation: ______________________

24. īstis

Person / Number: ______________________

Translation: ______________________

24. iērunt

Person / Number: ______________________

Translation: ______________________

The Present, Imperfect, Future, & Perfect Tense

Instructions: Read over each example and identify what tense, person, and number is for each Latin verb. Write your answers in the space provided under each verb.

Example: *studuistī*: Perfect Tense, Second Person, Singular, meaning "you studied."

1. veniō

Tense: ______________________________

Person & Number : ______________________________

Translation: ______________________________

2. portā**vit**

Tense: ______________________________

Person & Number : ______________________________

Translation: ______________________________

3. ambulā**bat**

Tense: ______________________________

Person & Number : ______________________________

Translation: ______________________________

4. habu**istī**

Tense: ______________________________

Person & Number : ______________________________

Translation: ______________________________

5. ambulā**bitis**

Tense: ______________________________

Person & Number : ______________________________

Translation: ______________________________

6. ambulā**mus**

Tense: ______________________________

Person & Number : ______________________________

Translation: ______________________________

7. ambulā**bat**

Tense: ______________________________

Person & Number : ______________________________

Translation: ______________________________

The Present, Imperfect, Future, & Perfect Tense

Instructions: Continue the exercise from the previous page.

8. ambulā**bātis**

Tense: ____________________

Person & Number : ____________________

Translation: ____________________

9. veni**am**

Tense: ____________________

Person & Number : ____________________

Translation: ____________________

10. veni**unt**

Tense: ____________________

Person & Number : ____________________

Translation: ____________________

11. vēn**īstis**

Tense: ____________________

Person & Number : ____________________

Translation: ____________________

12. leg***is***

Tense: ____________________

Person & Number : ____________________

Translation: ____________________

13. mīs**it**

Tense: ____________________

Person & Number : ____________________

Translation: ____________________

14. amāv**īmus**

Tense: ____________________

Person & Number : ____________________

Translation: ____________________

14. ambulā**tis**

Tense: ____________________

Person & Number : ____________________

Translation: ____________________

The Pluperfect Tense

LATIN HAS six tenses overall. Remember that the word *tense* refers to the time an action takes place, and the word *aspect* refers to the kind of action the verb is, whether the action is *ongoing* or *completed*. We have covered four of those six tenses, including the present tense, the imperfect tense, the future tense, and the perfect tense. The remaining two tenses are the pluperfect tense and the future perfect tense. Both of these tenses are formed from the **third principal part**, just like the perfect tense.

The pluperfect tense is literally a "more perfect tense." The prefix ***plu*** - added onto the word *perfect* is like our English *plus*, meaning "more." The **pluperfect tense** refers to a completed action that takes place before another action or event takes place. The pluperfect tense corresponds to the past perfect tense in English, a tense used for completed actions that took place before another action took place.

In translating the pluperfect tense, we almost always use the word *had*. For example, ***I had eaten lunch before I went to the Forum***; or ***Julius Caesar had invaded Britain before he crossed the Rhine River*** or ***Remus saw a flock of geese before Romulus saw an even larger flock of geese.***

As with the perfect tense, we form the pluperfect off of the third principal part. The third principal part is the first person singular, perfect tense form of a verb. Here are the four principal parts of four different verbs, plus the third principal part in larger and bolded font:

- *amō, amāre,* **amāvī**, *amatus:* to like, love
- *habeō, habēre,* **habuī**, *habitus:* to have, hold
- *mittō, mittere,* **mīsī**, *missus:* to send
- *audiō, audīre,* **audīvī**, *audītus:* to hear, listen

To form the perfect tense stem, we take the third principal part and remove the personal endings. If we took *amāvī*, we would remove the - *ī* to leave us with *amāv-*, our perfect tense stem. We add the following endings to make the pluperfect tense, which are - ***eram***, - ***erās***, - ***erat***, - ***erāmus***, - ***erātis***, - ***erant***. The diagram below shows forming a verb in the pluperfect tense.

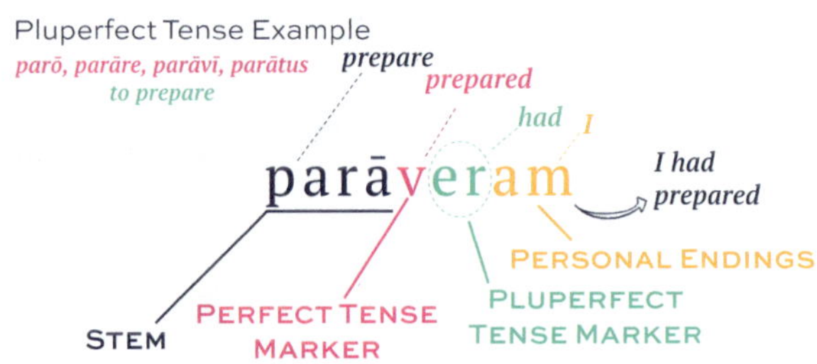

BIG IDEA

The pluperfect tense is literally the "more perfect" tense and describes a completed action that happened before another action happened in the sentence. The pluperfect tense is formed from the third principal part and has endings that look like the imperfect form of sum, esse*: -eram, -erās, -erat, -erāmus, -erātis, -erant. The pluperfect tense is translated with the helping verb "had."*

Review Vocabulary

Third Principal Part
The first person singular, perfect tense form of a verb.

Pluperfect Tense
A completed action that occurred before another verb in the sentence

Past Perfect Tense
In English, this tense refers to a completed action that took place in the past.

Perfect Tense
The perfect tense refers to a completed action that took place in the past.

Perfect Tense Markers
The perfect tense markers include the letters - i, - u, or - v and are found between the perfect tense stem and the personal endings.

You may have noticed the endings for the pluperfect tense look familiar. These endings are the same as the endings for the irregular verb *sum, esse* in the imperfect tense. If you have already memorized the imperfect tense endings for *sum, esse*, then you are halfway there to mastering the charts for the pluperfect tense. Here are the charts for verbs in the first, second, third, and fourth conjugations.

1st Conjugation *parō, parāre, parāvī, parātus:* to prepared	2nd Conjugation *moveō, movēre, mōvī, mōtus:* to move	3rd Conjugation *mittō, mittere, mīsī, missus:* to send	4th Conjugation *audiō, audīre, audīvī, audītus:* to listen, hear
parāveram / I had prepared	mōveram/ I had moved	mīseram /I had sent	audīveram / I had heard
parāverās / you had prepared	mōverās/ you had moved	mīserās / you had sent	audīverās / you had heard
parāverat / he, she, it had prepared	mōverat / he, she, it had moved	mīserat / he, she, it had sent	audīverat / he, she, it had heard
parāveramus we had prepared	mōveramus / we had moved	mīseramus / we had sent	audīveramus / we had heard
parāveratis / you (all) had prepared	mōveratis / you (all) had moved	mīseratis / you (all) had sent	audīveratis / you (all) had heard
parāverant / they had prepared	mōverant / they had moved	mīserant / they had sent	audīverant / they had heard

To summarize, the pluperfect tense is used for completed actions that took place before another action in the sentence took place. That is, we have two actions being expressed, and the pluperfect tense is used for actions that came before another action in the past. We use the auxiliary helping verb *had* to translate the pluperfect tense into English.

As with the perfect tense, the pluperfect tense is formed from the third principal part, or the first person singular, perfect tense form of a verb. Once we remove the personal ending from the third principal part, we can add the pluperfect endings onto the verb.

The pluperfect endings are *eram, erās, erat, eramus, eratis, erant*, which are identical to the imperfect tense forms of the verb *sum, esse*.

Lesson Review Questions

1. What is the pluperfect tense? What kind of actions does it express?

2. How do we translate the pluperfect tense?

3. How do we form the pluperfect tense?

4. The endings to the pluperfect tense look eerily similar to the form of what verb? in what tense?

The Pluperfect Tense / Practice

Instructions: Write the Latin Form in the first column and the English translation in the second column for each verb listed below in the perfect tense.

Person & Number	Example 1st Conjugation *parō, parāre, paravī, paratus* to prepare	Example 2nd Conjugation *moveō, movēre, movī, motus* to move
1st Person, Singular / I __		
2nd Person, Singular / you __		
3rd Person, Singular / he, she, it __		
1st Person, Plural / we __		
2nd Person, Plural / you (impl. pl.) __		
3rd Person, Plural / they __		

Person & Number	Example 3rd Conjugation Verb *legō, legere, lēgī, lectus* to read	Example 4th Conjugation Verb *audiō, audīre, audīvī, audītus* to listen
1st Person, Singular / I __		
2nd Person, Singular / you __		
3rd Person, Singular / he, she, it __		
1st Person, Plural / we __		
2nd Person, Plural / you (impl. pl.) __		
3rd Person, Plural / they __		

Sum, Possum, Volō, & Nōlō: Pluperfect Tense

An irregular verb is a verb that does not have a predictable, recognizable pattern.

The *pluperfect tense*, used for a completed action that will take place before another action takes place.

Tense, Person, & Number	sum, esse, fuī, futurus	possum, posse, potuī	volō, velle, voluī	eō, īre, itūrus
1st Person, Singular	fueram / I had been	potueram / I had been able to	volueram / I had wanted	ieram / I had gone
2nd Person, Singular	fuerās / you had been	potuerās / you had been able to	voluerās / you had wanted	ierās / you had gone
3rd Person, Singular	fuerat / he, she, it had been	potuerat / he, she, it had been able to	voluerat / he, she, it had wanted	ierat / he, she, it had gone
1st Person, Plural	fuerāmus / we had been	potuerāmus / we had been able to	voluerām / we had wanted	ierāmus / we had gone
2nd Person, Plural	fuerātis / you (all) had been	potuerātis / you (all) had been able to	voluerātis / you (all) had wanted	ierātis / you (all) had gone
3rd Person, Plural	fuerant / they had been	potuerant / they had been able to	voluerant/ they had wanted	ierant / they had gone

The Pluperfect Tense / Practice

Instructions: Write the Latin Form in the first column and the English translation in the second column for each verb listed below in the perfect tense.

Person & Number	Example Irregular Verb *sum, esse, fuī, futurus*: to be	Example Irregular Verb *possum, posse, potuī*: to be able to, can
1st Person, Singular		
2nd Person, Singular		
3rd Person, Singular		
1st Person, Plural		
2nd Person, Plural		
3rd Person, Plural		

Person & Number	Example Irregular Verb *volō, velle, voluī*: to want	Example Irregular Verb *eō, īre, itūrus*: to go
1st Person, Singular		
2nd Person, Singular		
3rd Person, Singular		
1st Person, Plural		
2nd Person, Plural		
3rd Person, Plural		

The Pluperfect Tense / Practice

Instructions: Please conjugate the following verbs in the *pluperfect* tense.

Conjugate & Translate: *laudō, -āre, -āvī, -ātus: to praise*

Conjugation: ______________________

Singular

1st Singular: ______________________

Translation: ______________________

2nd Singular: ______________________

Translation: ______________________

3rd Singular: ______________________

Translation: ______________________

Plural

1st Plural: ______________________

Translation: ______________________

2nd Plural: ______________________

Translation: ______________________

3rd Plural: ______________________

Translation: ______________________

Conjugate & Translate: sciō, scīre, scīvī, scītus, *to know*

Conjugation: ______________________

Singular

1st Singular: ______________________

Translation: ______________________

2nd Singular: ______________________

Translation: ______________________

3rd Singular: ______________________

Translation: ______________________

Plural

1st Plural: ______________________

Translation: ______________________

2nd Plural: ______________________

Translation: ______________________

3rd Plural: ______________________

Translation: ______________________

The Pluperfect Tense / Practice

Instructions: Please form the various forms for the *Pluperfect* tense of the following verbs.

Conjugate & Translate: *doceō, docēre, docuī, doctus*, to teach

Conjugation: ______________________________

Singular

1st Singular: ______________________________

Translation: ______________________________

2nd Singular: ______________________________

Translation: ______________________________

3rd Singular: ______________________________

Translation: ______________________________

Plural

1st Plural: ______________________________

Translation: ______________________________

2nd Plural: ______________________________

Translation: ______________________________

3rd Plural: ______________________________

Translation: ______________________________

Conjugate & Translate: *agō, agere, ēgī, āctum*: to do, drive

Conjugation: ______________________________

Singular

1st Singular: ______________________________

Translation: ______________________________

2nd Singular: ______________________________

Translation: ______________________________

3rd Singular: ______________________________

Translation: ______________________________

Plural

1st Plural: ______________________________

Translation: ______________________________

2nd Plural: ______________________________

Translation: ______________________________

3rd Plural: ______________________________

Translation: ______________________________

The Pluperfect Tense & Verb Persons

Instructions: Read over each example and identify the person and number for each Latin verb. Write your answers in the space provided under each verb. Translate the verb.

Verb #1: *ambulō, -āre, -āvī, -ātus: to walk*

1. ambulā**veram**

Person / Number: ____________________

Translation: ____________________

2. ambulā**verat**

Person / Number: ____________________

Translation: ____________________

3. ambulā**verant**

Person / Number: ____________________

Translation: ____________________

4. ambulā**verātis**

Translation: ____________________

Verb #2: *habeō, -ēre, -uī, -itus:* to have, to hold

5. habu**erāmus**

Person / Number: ____________________

Translation: ____________________

6. habu**erātis**

Person / Number: ____________________

Translation: ____________________

7. habu**erās**

Person / Number: ____________________

Translation: ____________________

8. habu**eram**

Person / Number: ____________________

Translation: ____________________

PRACTICE & REVIEW

The Pluperfect Tense & Verb Persons

Instructions: Continue the exercise from the previous page.

9. habu**erant**

Person / Number: ______________________________

Translation: ______________________________

10. habu**erat**

Person / Number: ______________________________

Translation: ______________________________

Verb #3: *veniō, venīre, vēnī, ventus:* to come

11. vēn**eram**

Person / Number: ______________________________

Translation: ______________________________

12. vēn**erātis**

Person / Number: ______________________________

Translation: ______________________________

13. vēn**erāmus**

Person / Number: ______________________________

Translation: ______________________________

14. vēn**erant**

Person / Number: ______________________________

Translation: ______________________________

15. vēn**erās**

Person / Number: ______________________________

Translation: ______________________________

16. vēn**erat**

Person / Number: ______________________________

Translation: ______________________________

The Present, Imperfect, Future, Perfect, & Pluperfect Tense

Instructions: Read over each example and identify what tense, person, and number is for each Latin verb. Write your answers in the space provided under each verb.

Example: *portāveramus*: Pluperfect, First Person, Plural, *we had carried*

1. veniō

Tense, Person, & Number: ______________________

Translation: ______________________

2. portāvit

Tense, Person, & Number: ______________________

Translation: ______________________

3. ambulābat

Tense, Person, & Number: ______________________

Translation: ______________________

4. habuerās

Tense, Person, & Number: ______________________

Translation: ______________________

5. ambulābitis

Tense, Person, & Number: ______________________

Translation: ______________________

6. ambulāmus

Tense, Person, & Number: ______________________

Translation: ______________________

7. ambulābat

Tense, Person, & Number: ______________________

Translation: ______________________

The Present, Imperfect, Future, Perfect, & Pluperfect Tense

Instructions: Continue the exercise from the previous page.

8. vēn**eratis**

Tense, Person, & Number: ____________________

Translation: ____________________

9. veni**ent**

Tense, Person, & Number: ____________________

Translation: ____________________

10. portāv**erant**

Tense, Person, & Number: ____________________

Translation: ____________________

11. vēn**īstis**

Tense, Person, & Number: ____________________

Translation: ____________________

12. leg***is***

Tense, Person, & Number: ____________________

Translation: ____________________

13. mīs**it**

Tense, Person, & Number: ____________________

Translation: ____________________

14. amāv**erās**

Tense, Person, & Number: ____________________

Translation: ____________________

14. ambulāv**erat**

Tense, Person, & Number: ____________________

Translation: ____________________

The Future Perfect Tense

THE SIXTH AND final tense is the future perfect tense. Remember that the word *tense* refers to the time an action takes place and the kind of action it is.

The **future perfect tense** is used for actions that will be completed in the future before another action takes place. (This tense has the same name in English.)We translate a verb in the future perfect tense with the auxiliary helping verb *will have*, as in the following examples. *I will have eaten lunch before I return from the Forum*; or *Brutus will have ousted the Tarquins before the Tarquins could cause any more trouble.* We should note that, at times, a verb in the future perfect tense is better translated as "have done" than "will have done."

As with the perfect tense and the pluperfect tense, we form the future perfect off of the third principal part, minus the *-i* ending. These forms appear below with the third principal part in larger, bold font:

- *parō, parāre,* **parāvī**, *paratus:* to prepare
- *habeō, habēre,* **habuī**, *habitus:* to have, hold
- *mittō, mittere,* **mīsī**, *missus:* to send
- *audiō, audīre,* **audīvī**, *audītus:* to hear, listen

We form the future perfect tense by starting with the perfect tense stem and removing the last letter (*-ī*), the first person singular ending. If we took *parāvī*, we remove the - *ī* to leave us with our stem, *parāv-*. Then we add the following endings to make the future perfect tense: *- erō, - eris, - erit, -erimus, -eritis, -erint*. The diagram below helps illustrate forming the future perfect tense.

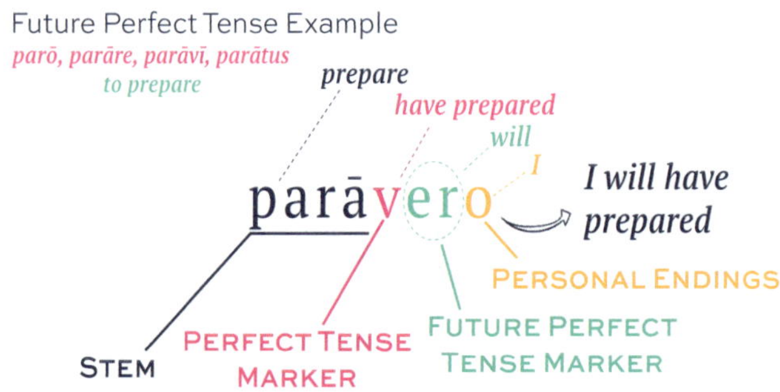

As with the pluperfect tense, the endings look similar to a chart you have already memorized. These endings are actually the same as the future tense endings for the irregular verb, *sum, esse*.

If you have memorized the future tense endings for *sum, esse*, then all you need to do is attach them to the third principal part, like the examples on the following page. Please note that the third person plural form is different in the future perfect than in the future form of *sum, esse*.

BIG IDEA

The future perfect tense describes an action that will be completed before some other action happens in the future. The future perfect tense is formed from the third principal part and has endings that look like the future tense form of sum, esse*: - erō, - eris, - erit, - erimus, - eritis, - erint. The future perfect tense is translated with the helping verb "will have."*

Vocabulary

Future Perfect Tense
An action that will be completed in the future before another action takes place.

Perfect Tense Markers
The perfect tense markers include the letters - *s*, - *u*, or - *v* and are found between the perfect tense stem and the personal endings.

1st Conjugation *parō, parāre, parāvī, parātus:* to prepare	2nd Conjugation *moveō, movēre, mōvī, mōtus:* to move	3rd Conjugation *mittō, mittere, mīsī, missus:* to send	4th Conjugation *audiō, audīre, audīvī, audītus:* to listen, hear
parāverō / I will have prepared	mōverō/ I will have moved	mīserō /I will have sent	audīverō / I will have heard
parāveris / you will have prepared	mōveris/ you will have moved	mīseris / you will have sent	audīveris / you will have heard
parāverit / he, she, it will have prepared	mōverit / he, she, it will have moved	mīserit / he, she, it will have sent	audīverit / he, she, it will have heard
parāverimus we will have prepared	mōverimus / we will have moved	mīserimus / we will have sent	audīverimus / we will have heard
parāveritis / you (all) will have prepared	mōveritis / you (all) will have moved	mīseritis / you (all) will have sent	audīveritis / you (all) will have heard
parāverint / they will have prepared	mōverint / they will have moved	mīserint / they will have sent	audīverint / they will have heard

Forming the future perfect tense is relatively straightforward once you know how to form the perfect tense and the pluperfect tense. In this case, we are adding a different set of endings to the perfect tense stem. Translating the future perfect is difficult, as the future perfect tense refers to actions that will be completed in the future but before another action takes place. We translate the future perfect tense with the helping verb "will have" to communicate the idea of a perfect action that has not taken place yet but most certainly will at some point in the future. But the future perfect tense is also the rarest tense in Latin.

To summarize, the future perfect tense is used for completed actions that will take place sometime in the future before another action. That is, the sentence has two actions being expressed, and the future perfect tense is used for actions that will take place before another action is completed later on in the future. We use the helping verbs *will* and *have* to translate the future perfect tense into English.

As with the perfect tense, the pluperfect tense is formed from the third principal part, which is the perfect tense or the first person singular, perfect tense form of a verb. Once we remove the personal ending from the third principal part, we can add the future perfect endings onto the verb. The future perfect endings are *- erō, - eris, - erit, - erimus, - eritis, - erint*, which are similar to the future tense forms of the verb *sum, esse*.

Lesson Review Questions

1. What is the future perfect tense? What kind of actions does it describe?

2. How do we translate the future perfect tense? What helping verbs do we use?

3. How do we form the future perfect tense?

4. The endings to the future perfect tense look eerily similar to the form of what verb? In what tense do we find those endings?

The Future Perfect Tense / Practice

Instructions: Conjugate the following verbs in the future perfect tense.

Person & Number	Example 1st Conjugation *laudō, laudāre, laudavī, laudatus: to praise*	Example 2nd Conjugation *teneō, tenēre, tenuī, tentus to hold*
1st Person, Singular		
2nd Person, Singular		
3rd Person, Singular		
1st Person, Plural		
2nd Person, Plural		
3rd Person, Plural		

Person & Number	Example 3rd Conjugation Verb *vēndō, vēndere, vēndidī, vēnditus:* to sell	Example 4th Conjugation Verb *sciō, scīre, scīvī, scītus:* to know
1st Person, Singular		
2nd Person, Singular		
3rd Person, Singular		
1st Person, Plural		
2nd Person, Plural		
3rd Person, Plural		

Sum, Possum, Volō, & Eō: Pluperfect & Future Perfect Tense

An irregular verb is a verb that does not have a predictable, recognizable pattern.

The *pluperfect tense*, used for a completed action that will take place before another action takes place.

Tense, Person, & Number	sum, esse, fuī, futurus	possum, posse, potuī	volō, velle, voluī	eō, īre, itūrus
Pluperfect, 1st Person, Singular	fueram / I had been	poteram / I had been able to	volueram / I had wanted	ieram / I had gone
Pluperfect, 2nd Person, Singular	fuerās / you had been	poterās / you had been able to	voluerās / you had wanted	ierās / you had gone
Pluperfect, 3rd Person, Singular	fuerat / he, she, it had been	poterat / he, she, it had been able to	voluerat / he, she, it had wanted	ierat / he, she, it had gone
Pluperfect, 1st Person, Plural	fuerāmus / we had been	poterāmus / we had been able to	voluerām / we had wanted	ierāmus / we had gone
Pluperfect, 2nd Person, Plural	fuerātis / you (all) had been	poterātis / you (all) had been able to	voluerātis / you (all) had wanted	ierātis / you (all) had gone
Pluperfect, 3rd Person, Plural	fuerant / they had been	poterant / they had been able to	voluerant/ they had wanted	ierant / they had gone
The *future perfect tense*, used for a completed action that will take place in the future.				
Future Perfect, 1st Person, Singular	fuerō / I will have been	poterō / I will have been able to	voluerō / I will have wanted	ierō / I will have gone
Future Perfect, 2nd Person, Singular	fueris / you will have been	poteris / you will have been able to	volueris / you will have wanted	ieris / you will have gone
Future Perfect, 3rd Person, Singular	fuerit / he, she, it will have been	poterit / he, she, it will have been able to	voluerit / he, she, it will have wanted	ierit / he, she, it will have gone
Future Perfect, 1st Person, Plural	fuerimus / we will have been	poterimus / we will have been able to	voluerimus / we will have wanted	ierimus / we will have gone
Future Perfect, 2nd Person, Plural	fueritis / you (all) will have been	poteritis / you (all) will have been able to	volueritis / you (all) will have wanted	ieritis / you (all) will have gone
Future Perfect, 3rd Person, Plural	fuerint / they will have been	poterint / they will have been able to	voluerint / they will have wanted	ierint / they will have gone

The Future Perfect Tense / Practice

Instructions: Conjugate the following verbs in the future perfect tense.

Person & Number	Example Irregular Verb *sum, esse, fuī, futurus*: to be	Example Irregular Verb *possum, posse, potuī*: to be able to, can
1st Person, Singular		
2nd Person, Singular		
3rd Person, Singular		
1st Person, Plural		
2nd Person, Plural		
3rd Person, Plural		

Person & Number	Example Irregular Verb *volō, velle, voluī*: to want	Example Irregular Verb *eō, īre, iī / ivī, itus*: to go
1st Person, Singular		
2nd Person, Singular		
3rd Person, Singular		
1st Person, Plural		
2nd Person, Plural		
3rd Person, Plural		

The Future Perfect Tense / Practice

Instructions: Please conjugate the following verbs in the future perfect tense.

Conjugate & Translate: *tangō, tangere, tetigī, tāctus*: to touch

Conjugation: ____________________

Singular

1st Singular: ____________________

Translation: ____________________

2nd Singular: ____________________

Translation: ____________________

3rd Singular: ____________________

Translation: ____________________

Plural

1st Plural: ____________________

Translation: ____________________

2nd Plural: ____________________

Translation: ____________________

3rd Plural: ____________________

Translation: ____________________

Conjugate & Translate: *videō, vidēre, vīdī, vīsus*, to see

Conjugation: ____________________

Singular

1st Singular: ____________________

Translation: ____________________

2nd Singular: ____________________

Translation: ____________________

3rd Singular: ____________________

Translation: ____________________

Plural

1st Plural: ____________________

Translation: ____________________

2nd Plural: ____________________

Translation: ____________________

3rd Plural: ____________________

Translation: ____________________

The Future Perfect Tense / Practice

Instructions: Please continue the exercise from the previous page.

Conjugate & Translate: *sedeō, sedēre, sēdī, sessum, to sit*

Conjugation: ______________________________

Singular

1st Singular: ______________________________

Translation: ______________________________

2nd Singular: ______________________________

Translation: ______________________________

3rd Singular: ______________________________

Translation: ______________________________

Plural

1st Plural: ______________________________

Translation: ______________________________

2nd Plural: ______________________________

Translation: ______________________________

3rd Plural: ______________________________

Translation: ______________________________

Conjugate & Translate: veniō, venīre, vēnī, ventus: to come

Conjugation: ______________________________

Singular

1st Singular: ______________________________

Translation: ______________________________

2nd Singular: ______________________________

Translation: ______________________________

3rd Singular: ______________________________

Translation: ______________________________

Plural

1st Plural: ______________________________

Translation: ______________________________

2nd Plural: ______________________________

Translation: ______________________________

3rd Plural: ______________________________

Translation: ______________________________

The Future Perfect Tense & Verb Persons

Instructions: Read over each sentence and identify the person and number for each Latin verb. Write your answers in the space provided under each verb. Then translate the verb.

Verb #1: ***ambulō, ambulāre, ambulāvī, ambulatus: to walk***

1. ambulā**verimus**

Person / Number: ______________________________

Translation: ______________________________

2. ambulā**verit**

Person / Number: ______________________________

Translation: ______________________________

3. ambulā**verint**

Person / Number: ______________________________

Translation: ______________________________

4. ambulā**veritis**

Translation: ______________________________

Verb #2: ***habeō, habēre, habuī, habitus:*** **to have, to hold**

5. habu**erimus**

Person / Number: ______________________________

Translation: ______________________________

6. habu**eritis**

Person / Number: ______________________________

Translation: ______________________________

7. habu**eris**

Person / Number: ______________________________

Translation: ______________________________

8. habu**erō**

Person / Number: ______________________________

Translation: ______________________________

The Future Perfect Tense & Verb Persons

Instructions: Continue the exercise from the previous page.

9. habu**erint**

Person / Number: ______________________________

Translation: ______________________________

10. habu**erit**

Person / Number: ______________________________

Translation: ______________________________

Verb #3: ***veniō, venīre, vēnī, ventus:*** **to come**

11. vēn**erō**

Person / Number: ______________________________

Translation: ______________________________

12. vēn**eritis**

Person / Number: ______________________________

Translation: ______________________________

13. vēn**erimus**

Person / Number: ______________________________

Translation: ______________________________

14. vēn**erint**

Person / Number: ______________________________

Translation: ______________________________

15. vēn**eris**

Person / Number: ______________________________

Translation: ______________________________

16. vēn**erit**

Person / Number: ______________________________

Translation: ______________________________

The Present, Imperfect, Future, Perfect, Pluperfect, & Future Perfect Tense

Instructions: Read over each example and identify what tense, person, and number is for each Latin verb. Write your answers in the space provided under each verb.

Example: ***portāverit*****: Future Perfect Tense, Third, Singular, meaning** ***I will have carried.***

1. habu**erō**

Tense, Person, & Number: ______________________

Translation: ______________________

2. portāv**it**

Tense, Person, & Number: ______________________

Translation: ______________________

3. ambulā**bat**

Tense, Person, & Number: ______________________

Translation: ______________________

4. habu**erās**

Tense, Person, & Number: ______________________

Translation: ______________________

5. ambulā**bitis**

Tense, Person, & Number: ______________________

Translation: ______________________

6. ambulā**mus**

Tense, Person, & Number: ______________________

Translation: ______________________

7. ambulā**bat**

Tense, Person, & Number: ______________________

Translation: ______________________

8. vēn**eratis**

Tense, Person, & Number: ______________________

Translation: ______________________

9. veni**ent**

Tense, Person, & Number: ______________________

Translation: ______________________

Practice & Review

The Present, Imperfect, Future, Perfect, Pluperfect, & Future Perfect Tense

Instructions: Read over each example and identify what tense, person, and number is for each Latin verb. Write your answers in the space provided under each verb.

10. portā**verant**

Tense, Person, & Number: ____________________

Translation: ______________________________

11. vēn**īstis**

Tense, Person, & Number: ____________________

Translation: ______________________________

12. leg**is**

Tense, Person, & Number: ____________________

Translation: ______________________________

13. mīs**it**

Tense, Person, & Number: ____________________

Translation: ______________________________

14. vēn**erō**

Tense, Person, & Number: ____________________

Translation: ______________________________

14. ambulā**verat**

Tense, Person, & Number: ____________________

Translation: ______________________________

15. amāv**istī**

Tense, Person, & Number: ____________________

Translation: ______________________________

16. portāv**erō**

Tense, Person, & Number: ____________________

Translation: ______________________________

17. ambulā**bātis**

Tense, Person, & Number: ____________________

Translation: ______________________________

18. leg**unt**

Tense, Person, & Number: ____________________

Translation: ______________________________

PANTHEON / INTERIOR

Photo by Julie (Unsplash)

Appendix I
Paradigm Charts

CHARTS

Latin Paradigms: First & Second Declensions

Latin is an inflected language, meaning that the last 1 to 4 letters of each Latin noun provide important information about how that noun is used in a sentence. Below is the chart for *Latin Nouns* for the *First* and *Second* declensions.

Singular Nouns / *The noun refers to only one person, place, or thing.*

Case	1st Declension Feminine	2nd Declension Masculine	2nd Declension Masculine	2nd Declension Neuter
Nominative Case *Subjects*	puella / a, the girl	puer / a, the boy	hortus / a, the garden	caelum / the heaven
Genitive Case *Possession*	puellae / of the girl	puerī / of the boy	hortī / of the garden	caelī / of the heaven
Dative Case *Indirect Objects*	puellae / to *or* for the girl	puerō / to *or* for the boy	hortō / to *or* for the garden	caelō / to *or* for heaven
Accusative Case *Direct Objects*	puellam a / the girl	puerum / a, the boy	hortum / a, the garden	caelum / the heaven
Ablative Case *Object of a Preposition*	puellā / by, with, or from the girl	puerō / by, with, or from the boy	hortō / by, with, or from the garden	caelō / by, with, or from the heaven
Vocative Case *Direct Address*	puella / oh, girl	puer / oh, boy	horte / oh, garden	caelum / oh, heaven

Plural Nouns / *The noun refers to two (or more) people, places, or things.*

Case	1st Declension Feminine	2nd Declension Masculine	2nd Declension Masculine	2nd Declension Neuter
Nominative Case *Subjects*	puellae / the girls	puerī / the boys	hortī / the gardens	caela / the heavens
Genitive Case *Possession*	puellārum / of the girls	puerōrum / of the boys	hortōrum / of the gardens	caelōrum / of the heavens
Dative Case *Indirect Objects*	puellīs / to *or* for the girls	puerīs / to *or* for the boys	hortīs / to *or* for the gardens	caelīs / to *or* for the heavens
Accusative Case *Direct Objects*	puellās / the girls	puerōs / the boys	hortōs / the gardens	caela / the heavens
Ablative Case *Object of a Preposition*	puellīs / by, with, or from the girls	puerīs / by, with, or from the boys	hortīs / by, with, or from the gardens	caelīs / by, with, or from the heavens
Vocative Case *Direct Address*	puellae / oh, girls	puerī / oh, boys	hortī / oh, gardens	caela / oh, heavens

Latin Paradigms: Third Declension

Below is the chart for *Latin Nouns* for the *Third* declension.

Singular Nouns / *The noun refers to only one person, place, or thing.*

Case	3rd Declension Masculine	3rd Declension Feminine	3rd Declension Neuter	3rd Declension (i-stem)
Nominative Case *Subjects*	pater* / a, the father	māter* / a, the mother	nōmen* / a, the name	ars* / a, the art
Genitive Case *Possession*	patris / of the father	mātris / of the mother	nōminis / of the name	artis / of the art
Dative Case *Indirect Objects*	patrī / to *or* for the father	mātrī / to *or* for the mother	nōminī / to *or* for the name	artī / to *or* for the art
Accusative Case *Direct Objects*	patrem / a, the father	mātrem / a, the mother	nōmen / a, the name	artem / a, the art
Ablative Case *Object of a Preposition*	patre / by, with, or from the father	mātre / by, with, or from the mother	nōmine / by, with, or from the name	arte / by, with, or from the art
Vocative Case *Direct Address*	pater/ oh, father	māter / oh, mother	nōmen / oh, name	ars / oh, art

Plural Nouns / *The noun refers to two (or more) people, places, or things.*

Case	3rd Declension Masculine	3rd Declension Feminine	3rd Declension Neuter	3rd Declension (i-stem)
Nominative Case *Subjects*	patrēs / the fathers	mātrēs / the mothers	nōmina / the names	artēs / the arts
Genitive Case *Possession*	patrum / of the fathers	mātrum / of the mothers	nōminum / of the names	artium / of the arts
Dative Case *Indirect Objects*	patribus / to *or* for the fathers	mātribus / to *or* for the mothers	nōminibus / to *or* for the names	artibus / to *or* for the arts
Accusative Case *Direct Objects*	patrēs / the fathers	mātrēs / the mothers	nōmina / the names	artēs / the arts
Ablative Case *Object of a Preposition*	patribus/ by, with, or from the fathers	mātribus/ by, with, or from the mothers	nōminibus / by, with, or from the names	artibus/ by, with, or from the arts
Vocative Case *Direct Address*	patrēs/ oh, fathers	mātrēs/ oh, mothers	nōmina / oh, names	artēs/ oh, arts

**Please note that the nominative singular form for the third declension is irregular. Therefore, the nominative singular form of each 3rd declension word must be memorized in order to recognize it.*

Latin Paradigms: First and Second Declension Adjectives

An adjective is a word that *modifies* or provides more information about another noun. In English, we know an adjective modifies another noun if that adjective is placed next to that noun. In Latin, that adjective has to agree in case, number, and gender with the noun that it modifies.

Singular Adjectives / *The adjective modifies one person, place, or thing.*

Case	magnus (m.)	magna (f.)	magnum (n.)
Nominative Case *Subjects*	magnus / a, the large one	magna / a, the large (one)	magnum / a, the large (one)
Genitive Case *Possession*	magnī / of the large (one)	magnae / of the large (one)	magnī / of the large (one)
Dative Case *Indirect Objects*	magnō / to *or* for the large (one)	magnae / to *or* for the large (one)	magnō / to *or* for the large (one)
Accusative Case *Direct Objects*	magnum / a, the large (one)	magnam a / the large (one)	magnum / a, the large (one)
Ablative Case *Object of a Preposition*	magnō / by, with, or from the large (one)	magnā / by, with, or from the large (one)	magnō / by, with, or from the large (one)
Vocative Case *Direct Address*	magne / oh, large (one)	magna / oh, large (one)	magnum / oh, large (one)

Plural Adjectives / *The adjective modifies two or more people, places, or things.*

Case	magnus (m.)	magna (f.)	magnum (n.)
Nominative Case *Subjects*	magnī / the large (ones)	magnae / a, the large (ones)	magna / the large (ones)
Genitive Case *Possession*	magnōrum / of the large (ones)	magnārum / of the large (ones)	magnōrum / of the large (ones)
Dative Case *Indirect Objects*	magnīs / to *or* for the large (ones)	magnīs / to *or* for the large (ones)	magnīs / to *or* for the large (ones)
Accusative Case *Direct Objects*	magnōs / the large (ones)	magnās / the large (ones)	magna / the large (ones)
Ablative Case *Object of a Preposition*	magnīs / by, with, or from the large (ones)	magnīs / by, with, or from the large (ones)	magnīs / by, with, *or* from the large (ones)
Vocative Case *Direct Address*	magnī / oh, large (ones)	magnae / oh, large (ones)	magna / oh, large (ones)

Latin Paradigms: Third Declension Adjectives

An adjective is a word that *modifies* or provides more information about another noun. In English, we know an adjective modifies another noun if that adjective is placed next to that noun. In Latin, that adjective has to agree in case, number, and gender with the noun that it modifies.

Singular Adjectives / *The adjective modifies one person, place, or thing.*			
Case	**fortis (m.)**	**fortis (f.)**	**forte (n.)**
Nominative Case *Subjects*	fortis / a, the brave (one)	fortis / a, the brave (one)	forte / a, the brave (one)
Genitive Case *Possession*	fortis / of the brave (one)	fortis / of the brave (one)	fortis / of the brave (one)
Dative Case *Indirect Objects*	fortī / to *or* for the brave (one)	fortī / to *or* for the brave (one)	fortī / to *or* for the brave (one)
Accusative Case *Direct Objects*	fortem / a, the brave (one)	fortem / a, the brave (one)	forte / a, the brave (one)
Ablative Case *Object of a Preposition*	fortī / by, with, or from the brave (one)	fortī / by, with, or from the brave (one)	fortī / by, with, or from the brave (one)
Vocative Case *Direct Address*	fortis / oh, brave (one)	fortis / oh, brave (one)	forte / oh, brave (one)
Plural Adjectives / *The adjective modifies two or more people, places, or things.*			
Nominative Case *Subjects*	fortēs / the brave (ones)	fortēs / the brave (ones)	fortia / the brave (ones)
Genitive Case *Possession*	fortium / of the brave (ones)	fortium / of the brave (ones)	fortium / of the brave (ones)
Dative Case *Indirect Objects*	fortibus / to *or* for the brave (ones)	fortibus / to *or* for the brave (ones)	fortibus / to *or* for the brave (ones)
Accusative Case *Direct Objects*	fortēs / the brave (ones)	fortēs / the brave (ones)	fortia / the brave (ones)
Ablative Case *Object of a Preposition*	fortibus / by, with, or from the brave (ones)	fortibus / by, with, or from the brave (ones)	fortibus / by, with, or from the brave (ones)
Vocative Case *Direct Address*	fortēs / oh, brave (ones)	fortēs / oh, brave (ones)	fortia / oh, brave (ones)

Latin Charts: Infinitives, Imperatives, & the Present Tense

Person & Number	1st Conjugation	2nd Conjugation	3rd Conjugation	4th Conjugation
Infinitive / *to* ________	parāre / to prepare	movēre / to move	mittere / to send	audīre / to hear
Imperative / Singular / Positive *A command to one person*	parā / (you) prepare	movē / (you) move	mitte / (you) send	audī / (you) hear
Imperative / Plural / Positive *A command to two or more people*	parāte / (you all) prepare	movēte / (you all) move	mittite (you all) send	audīte / (you all)hear
Imperative / Singular / Negative *A command to one person to not do something*	nōlī parāre / (you) don't prepare	nōlī movēre / (you) don't move	nōlī mittere / (you) don't send	nōlī audīre / (you) don't hear
Imperative / Plural / Negative *A command to two or more people to not do something*	nōlīte parāre / (you all) don't prepare	nōlīte movēre / (you all) don't move	nōlīte mittere / (you all) don't send	nōlīte audīre / (you all) don't hear
Present Tense / *The verb refers to an action currently occurring and is ongoing.*				
1st Person, Singular / *I*__	parō / I prepare, am preparing	moveō / I move, am moving	mittō / I send, am sending	audiō / I hear, am hearing
2nd Person, Singular / *you*__	parās / you prepare, are preparing	movēs / you move, are moving	mittis / you send, are sending	audīs / you hear, are hearing
3rd Person, Singular / *he, she, it*__	parat / he, she, it prepares, is preparing	movet / he, she, it moves, is moving	mittit / he, she, it sends, is sending	audit / he, she, it hear, is hearing
1st Person, Plural / *we*__	parāmus / we prepare, are preparing	movēmus / we move, are moving	mittimus / we send, are sending	audīmus / we hear, are hearing
2nd Person, Plural / *you (impl. pl.)*__	parātis / you (all) prepare, are preparing	movētis / you (all) move, are moving	mittitis / you (all) send, are sending	audītis / you (all) hear, are hearing
3rd Person, Plural / *they*__	parant / they prepare, are preparing	movent / they move, are moving	mittunt / they send, are sending	audiunt / they hear, are hearing

Latin Charts: The Imperfect & Future Tense

Person & Number	1st Conjugation	2nd Conjugation	3rd Conjugation	4th Conjugation
Infinitive / *to* ________	parāre / to prepare	movēre / to move	mittere / to send	audīre / to hear
Imperfect Tense / *The verb refers to an ongoing, habitual action which began in the past.*				
1st Person, Singular / *I*	parābam / I was preparing	movēbam / I was moving	mittēbam / I was sending	audiēbam / I was hearing
2nd Person, Singular / *you*	parābās / you were preparing	movēbās / you were moving	mittēbās / you were sending	audiēbās / you were hearing
3rd Person, Singular / *he, she, it* ___	parābat / he, she, it was preparing	movēbat / he, she, it was moving	mittēbat / he, she, it was sending	audiēbat / he, she, it was hearing
1st Person, Plural / *we*	parābāmus / we were preparing	movēbāmus / we were moving	mittēbāmus / we were sending	audiēbāmus / we were hearing
2nd Person, Plural / *you (impl. pl.)*	parābātis / you (all) were preparing	movēbātis / you (all) were moving	mittēbātis / you (all) were sending	audiēbātis / you (all) were hearing
3rd Person, Plural / *they*	parābant / they were preparing	movēbant / they were moving	mittēbant / they were sending	audiēbant / they were hearing
Future Tense / *The verb refers to an action that will happen in the future.*				
1st Person, Singular / *I*	parābō / I will prepare	movēbō / I will move	mittam / I will send	audiam / I will hear
2nd Person, Singular / *you*	parābis / you will prepare	movēbis / you will move	mittēs / you will send	audiēs / you will hear
3rd Person, Singular / *he, she, it* ___	parābit / he, she, it will prepare	movēbit / he, she, it will move	mittet / he, she, it will send	audiēt / he, she, it will hear
1st Person, Plural / *we*	parābimus / we will prepare	movēbimus / we will move	mittēmus / we will send	audiēmus / we will hear
2nd Person, Plural / *you (impl. pl.)*	parābitis / you (all) will prepare	movēbitis/ you (all) will move	mittētis / you (all) will send	audiētis/ you (all) will hear
3rd Person, Plural / *they*	parābunt / they will prepare	movēbunt / they will move	mittent / they will send	audient / they will hear

Latin Charts: Principal Parts & Perfect Tense

Person & Number	1st Conjugation	2nd Conjugation	3rd Conjugation	4th Conjugation
Dictionary Definition / *Latin dictionaries contain the four* **Principal Parts** *of a verb, listed below.*	parō, parāre, parāvī, parātus / to prepare	moveō, movēre, mōvī, mōtus / to move	mittō, mittere, mīsī, missus / to send	audiō, audīre, audīvī, audītus / to hear
First Principle Part / *Present Tense, First Person Singular*	parō / I am preparing	moveō / I move	mittō / I send	audiō / I hear
Second Principle Part / *Present Active Infinitive*	parāre / to prepare	movēre / to move	mittere / to send	audīre / to hear
Third Principle Part / *Perfect Tense, First Person Singular*	parāvī / I prepared	mōvī / I moved	mīsī / I sent	audīvī / I heard
Fourth Principle Part / *Perfect Passive Participle*	parātus, - a, - um / having been pre-pared	mōtus, - a, - um / having been moved	missus, - a, - um / having been sent	audītus, - a, - um / having been heard
Perfect Tense / *The verb refers to a past action and is not ongoing; in that sense, it is complete.*				
1st Person, Singular / *I*	parāvī / I prepared	mōvī / I moved	mīsī / I sent	audīvī / I heard
2nd Person, Singular / *you*	parāvistī / you prepared	mōvistī / you moved	mīsistī / you sent	audīvistī / you heard
3rd Person, Singular / *he, she, it*	parāvit / he, she, it prepared	mōvit / he, she, it moved	mīsit / he, she, it sent	audīvit / he, she, it heard
1st Person, Plural / *we*	parāvimus / we prepared	mōvimus / we moved	mīsimus / we sent	audīvimus / we heard
2nd Person, Plural / *you (impl. pl.)*	parāvistis / you (all) prepared	mōvistis / you (all) moved	mīsistis / you (all) sent	audīvistis / you (all) heard
3rd Person, Plural / *they*	parāvērunt / they prepared	mōvērunt / they moved	mīsērunt / they sent	audīvērunt / they heard

Latin Charts: Pluperfect & Future Perfect Tense

Person & Number	1st Conjugation	2nd Conjugation	3rd Conjugation	4th Conjugation
Dictionary Definition / *Latin dictionaries contain the four* **Principal Parts** *of a verb, listed below.*	parō, parāre, parāvī, parātus / to prepare	moveō, movēre, mōvī, mōtus / to move	mittō, mittere, mīsī, missus / to send	audiō, audīre, audīvī, audītus / to hear
Pluperfect Tense / *The verb refers to an action that took place at a definite point in the past.*				
1st Person, Singular / *I*	parāveram / I had prepared	mōveram / I had moved	mīseram / I had sent	audīveram / I had heard
2nd Person, Singular / *you*	parāverās / you had prepared	mōverās / you had moved	mīserās/ you had sent	audīverās / you had heard
3rd Person, Singular / *he, she, it___*	parāverat / he, she, it had prepared	mōverat / he, she, it had moved	mīserat / he, she, it had sent	audīverat / he, she, it had heard
1st Person, Plural / *we*	parāverāmus / we had prepared	mōverāmus / we had moved	mīserāmus / we had sent	audīverāmus / we had heard
2nd Person, Plural / *you (impl. pl.)*	parāverātis / you (all) had prepared	mōverātis / you (all) had moved	mīserātis / you (all) had sent	audīverātis / you (all) had heard
3rd Person, Plural / *they*	parāverant / they had prepared	mōverant / they had moved	mīserant / they had sent	audīverant / they had heard
Future Perfect Tense / *The verb refers to an action that will take place at a definite point in the future.*				
1st Person, Singular / *I*	parāverō / I will have prepared	mōverō/ I will have moved	mīserō / I will have sent	audīverō / I will have heard
2nd Person, Singular / *you*	parāveris / you will have prepared	mōveris / you will have moved	mīseris / you will have sent	audīveris / you will have heard
3rd Person, Singular / *he, she, it___*	parāverit / he, she, it will have prepared	mōverit / he, she, it will have moved	mīserit / he, she, it will have sent	audīverit / he, she, it will have heard
1st Person, Plural / *we*	parāverimus / we will have prepared	mōverimus / we will have moved	mīserimus / we will have sent	audīverimus / we will have heard
2nd Person, Plural / *you (impl. pl.)*	parāveritis / you (all) will have prepared	mōveritis / you (all) will have moved	mīseritis / you (all) will have sent	audīveritis / you (all) will have heard
3rd Person, Plural / *they*	parāverint / they will have prepared	mōverint / they will have moved	mīserint / they will have sent	audīverint / they will have heard

Sum, Possum, Volō, & Nōlō: Present & Imperfect Tense

An irregular verb is a verb that does not have a predictable, recognizeable pattern.

Tense, Person, & Number	sum, esse, fuī, futurus	possum, posse, potuī, futurus	volō, velle, voluī	nōlō, nōlle, nōluī
Infinitive / to ______	esse / to be	posse / to be able to do something, can	velle / to want	nōlle / to not want, wish
Present, 1st Person, Singular	sum / I am	possum / I can	volō / I want, wish	nōlō / I do not want, wish
Present, 2nd Person, Singular	es / you are	potes / you are	vīs / you want, wish	nōn vīs / you do not want, wish
Present, 3rd Person, Singular	est / he, she, it is	potest / he, she, it is	vult / he, she, it wants, wishes	nōn vult / he, she, it does not want, wish
Present, 1st Person, Plural	sumus / we are	possumus / we can	volumus / we want, wish	nōlumus / we do not want, wish
Present, 2nd Person, Plural	estis / you (all) are	potestis / you (all) can	vultis / you (all) want, wish	nōn vultis / you (all) do not want, wish
Present, 3rd Person, Plural	sunt / they are	possunt / they can	volunt / they want, wish	nōlunt / they do not want, wish
Imperfect, 1st Person, Singular	eram / I was	poteram / I was able to	volēbam / I was wanting, wishing	nōlēbam / I was not wanting, wishing
Imperfect, 2nd Person, Singular	erās / you were	poterās / you were able to	volēbās / you were wanting, wishing	nōlēbās / you were not wanting, wishing
Imperfect, 3rd Person, Singular	erat / he, she, it was	poterat / he, she, it were able to	volēbat / he, she, it was wanting, wishing	nōlēbat / he, she, it was not wanting, wishing
Imperfect, 1st Person, Plural	erāmus / we were	poterāmus / we were able to	volēbāmus / we were wanting, wishing	nōlēbāmus / we were not wanting, wishing
Imperfect, 2nd Person, Plural	erātis / you (all) were	poterātis / you (all) were able to	volēbātis / you (all) were wanting, wishing	nōlēbātis / you (all) were not wanting, wishing
Imperfect, 3rd Person, Plural	erant / they were	poterant / they were able to	volēbant / they were wanting, wishing	nōlēbant / they were not wanting, wishing

Sum, Possum, Volō, & Nōlō: Future & Perfect Tense

An irregular verb is a verb that does not have a predictable, recognizable pattern.

Tense, Person, & Number	sum, esse, fuī, futurus	possum, posse, potuī, futurus	volō, velle, voluī	nolō, nolle, noluī
Future, 1st Person, Singular	erō / I will be	poterō / I will be able to	volam / I will want, wish	nōlam / I will not want, wish
Future, 2nd Person, Singular	eris / you will be	poteris / you will be able to	volēs / you will want, wish	nōlēs / you will not want, wish
Future, 3rd Person, Singular	erit / he, she, it will be	poterit / he, she, it will be able to	volet / he, she, it will want, wish	nōlet / he, she, it will not want, wish
Future, 1st Person, Plural	erimus / we will be	poterimus / we will be able to	volēmus / we will want, wish	nōlēmus / we will not want, wish
Future, 2nd Person, Plural	eritis / you (all) will be	poteritis / you (all) will be able to	volētis / you (all) will want, wish	nōlētis / you (all) will not want, wish
Future, 3rd Person, Plural	erunt / they will be	poterunt / they will be able to	volent / they will want, wish	nōlent / they will not want, wish
Perfect, 1st Person, Singular	fuī / I was, I have been	potuī / I was able to, have been able to	voluī / I wanted	nōluī / I did not want
Perfect, 2nd Person, Singular	fuistī / you were, you have been	potuistī / you were able to, have been able to	voluistī / you wanted	nōluistī / you did not want
Perfect, 3rd Person, Singular	fuit / he, she, it was, has been	potuit / he, she, it was able to, has been able to	voluit / he, she, it wanted	nōluit / he, she, it did not want
Perfect, 1st Person, Plural	fuimus / we were, we have been	potuimus / we were able to, have been able to	voluimus / we wanted	nōluimus / we did not want
Perfect, 2nd Person, Plural	fuistis / you (all) were, you (all) have been	potuistis / you (all) were able to, have been able to	voluistis / you (all) wanted	nōluistis / you (all) did not want
Perfect, 3rd Person, Plural	fuērunt / they were, they have been	potuērunt / they were able to, have been able to	voluērunt / they wanted	nōluērunt / they did not want

Sum, Possum, Volō, & Nōlō: Pluperfect & Future Perfect Tense

An irregular verb is a verb that does not have a predictable, recognizable pattern.

The *pluperfect tense*, used for a completed action taking place before another action.

Tense, Person, & Number	sum, esse, fuī, futurus	possum, posse, potuī, futurus	volō, velle, voluī	nolō, nolle, noluī
Pluperfect, 1st Person, Singular	fueram / I had been	potueram / I had been able to	volueram / I had wanted	nōlueram / I had not wanted
Pluperfect, 2nd Person, Singular	fuerās / you had been	potuerās / you had been able to	voluerās / you had wanted	nōluerās / you had not wanted
Pluperfect, 3rd Person, Singular	fuerat / he, she, it had been	potuerat / he, she, it had been able to	voluerat / he, she, it had wanted	nōluerat/ he, she, it had not wanted
Pluperfect, 1st Person, Plural	fuerāmus / we had been	potuerāmus / we had been able to	voluerāmus / we had wanted	nōluerāmus / we had not wanted
Pluperfect, 2nd Person, Plural	fuerātis / you (all) had been	potuerātis / you (all) had been able to	voluerātis / you (all) had wanted	nōluerātis / you (all) had not wanted
Pluperfect, 3rd Person, Plural	fuerant / they had been	potuerant / they had been able to	voluerant / they had wanted	nōluerant / they had not wanted
The *future perfect tense*, used for a completed action that will take place in the future.				
Future Perfect, 1st Person, Singular	fuerō / I will have been	potuerō / I will have been able to	voluerō / I will have wanted	nōluerō / I will not have wanted
Future Perfect, 2nd Person, Singular	fueris / you will have been	potueris / you will have been able to	volueris / you will have wanted	nōlueris / you will not have wanted
Future Perfect, 3rd Person, Singular	fuerit / he, she, it will have been	potuerit / he, she, it will have been able to	voluerit / he, she, it will have wanted	nōluerit / he, she, it will not have wanted
Future Perfect, 1st Person, Plural	fuerimus / we will have been	potuerimus / we will have been able to	voluerimus / we will have wanted	nōluerimus / we will not have wanted
Future Perfect, 2nd Person, Plural	fueritis / you (all) will have been	potueritis / you (all) will have been able to	volueritis / you (all) will have wanted	nōlueritis / you (all) will not have wanted
Future Perfect, 3rd Person, Plural	fuerint / they will have been	potuerint / they will have been able to	voluerint / they will have wanted	nōluerint / they will not have wanted

NEVER ✦ CEASE
LEARNING

Made in the USA
Columbia, SC
06 July 2025

60037312R10087